Joyously through the Days

Wisdom Publications
199 Elm Street
Somerville MA 02144 USA
www.wisdompubs.org

Library of Congress Cataloging-in-Publication Data
Kaye, Les.
 Joyously through the days : living the journey of spiritual practice / Les Kaye ; Foreword by Huston Smith.
   pages cm
 Includes index.
 ISBN 0-86171-681-7 (pbk. : alk. paper)
 1. Religious life—Zen Buddhism. I. Smith, Huston, 1919– II. Title.
 BQ9286.2.K39 2011
 294.3'444—dc22

                            2010052127

15 14 13 12 11
5 4 3 2 1

ISBN 978-08-6171-681-4
eBook ISBN 978-086171-619-7

Cover design by Phil Pascuzzo. Interior design by TL. Set in Sabon 11/15.
Cover photograph : iStock.com

Joyously THROUGH THE DAYS

LIVING THE JOURNEY OF SPIRITUAL PRACTICE

Les Kaye
Foreword by Huston Smith

Wisdom Publications • Boston

To my wife Mary
whose warm heart raises blossoms
in all things.

CONTENTS

CONTENTS

FOREWORD

In his preface to this book, Les Kaye tells us that his "primary purpose in writing this book is to illustrate how Zen practice enhances awareness, patience, and generosity, and enables us to respond creatively to the complexities, distractions, and uncertainties of modern times." This is such an inspiring and pulse-quickening objective that I can think of no better way to begin my foreword than to highlight and underscore those four objectives.

I must have still been in my teens when a verse came my way—a prayer for awareness—that impacted me so forcefully that I still remember it today (even if not quite correctly). Much later, I learned this was part of a poem by Miriam Teichner:

> [Please], let me be aware.
> Let me not stumble blindly down the
>   ways,

Just getting somehow safely through the
    days.
Not even groping for another hand,
Not wondering why it all was planned, [...]
Please, keep me eager to do my share.
[Please], let me be aware.

This, I believe, is the awareness that Les Kaye points
to in this book. So how do we get to this continual
awareness? Teresa of Avila has said, "Patience attains
the goal." And the Zen that Les presents here is itself
a path to that goal-attaining patience. Generosity, the
third quality that Zen can enhance, is at its heart
capacity to empathize: to place oneself in another's
position; or (as the Native Americans put it) "walk a
mile in his moccasins."

The fourth benefit of Zen as Les Kaye presents it—
that it helps us "to respond creatively to the complexities, distractions, and uncertainties of our lives"—is
so clear that I do not have to explain or nuance it. Any
book—like this one—that can deliver on that prospect
should be kept close by one's side throughout the day.

Every abstract point is followed by examples and
anecdotes, some contemporary and others that are
drawn from history or literature. And the problems
the book touches on and seeks to allay reads like a
shopping list of our own daily woes. In addition, Les
Kaye's book points out skillfully many of our human
foibles—so familiar that they often seem to come too

close for comfort. At one point I found myself exclaiming, almost out loud, "How does he know me so well?"

This is a wise, practical, and inspiring book. For me, its value is enhanced by knowing that its author knows what he is talking about and works diligently at walking that talk.

Huston Smith
Berkeley, California

PREFACE

*In the greatest confusion there is still an open
channel to the soul. It may be difficult to find
because by midlife it is overgrown, and some of
the wildest thickets that surround it grow out
of what we describe as our education. But the
channel is always there, and it is our business to
keep it open, to have access to the deepest part
of ourselves—to that part of us which is
conscious of a higher consciousness, by means
of which we make final judgments and put
everything together.*

—Saul Bellow

My primary purpose in writing this book is to
illustrate how spiritual practice enhances
awareness, patience, and generosity, and
enables us to respond creatively to the complexities, distractions, and uncertainties of our lives. This collection

is based on reflections of forty years experiencing and observing the relevance of my own spiritual practice to the everyday world of family and work. In my case, my spiritual practice comes from the Zen tradition, and I have come to see the innumerable ways meditation brings balance, understanding, and a confident approach to the pressure cooker of our lives.

For me, Zen practice points to our inherent spirituality, the problems we create when we lose touch with it, and how we can regain it.

I hope these reflections illustrate how the spiritual and the ordinary converge continually—not merely once in a while.

I would like to thank my editor at Wisdom Publications, Josh Bartok, for his dedication to this project and for his insight that untangled so many knots.

SOURCES OF DIFFICULTY

ORIGINAL FOOLISHNESS

There is a story about a man and a horse. The horse is galloping quickly, and it appears that the man on the horse is going somewhere important. Another man, standing alongside the road, shouts, "Where are you going?" And the first man replies,
"I don't know! Ask the horse!"
—*Thich Nhat Hanh*

Buddhism understands humanity's source of unhappiness not as willful disobedience to a stern God but as foolishness arising from the never-ending desire for *just one more thing*. This very human tendency is so often what get us into trouble—as I vividly came to understand more than twenty years ago on a warm, summer morning.

I was in traffic school, in a crowded classroom of the County Social Services Agency building because I did something foolish two weeks earlier on a quiet country road. Approaching a stop sign with no traffic in sight, failing to spot the sheriff's well-hidden patrol car, I slowed but did not come to a complete stop. Had the maneuver worked, I would have saved perhaps five seconds and the "trouble" of shifting gears. Instead, my desire to save those few moments cost me $150 and a day in a crowded, stuffy classroom.

At the start, the instructor asked each of us to explain what had brought us to traffic school: where, when, and why we had done what we did. Our stories were an unfolding narrative of collective foolishness. I soon realized that I was in a room with fifty foolish people like myself who had also attempted an unwise tradeoff.

At any given moment, we can slip into doing something foolish. Almost impossible to avoid, this simply comes with being human. Sometimes it's a small thing we do or say, sometimes something larger. Sometimes we do it from misunderstanding a situation, sometimes from poor judgment—as in, "I can get away with it"—and sometimes because we get distracted. Nevertheless, though we are often foolish, we each have within us a great store of wisdom.

Zen's most profound teaching rests on the insight that everyone is originally a buddha, but we fail to recognize this foundational quality of our true nature due to our "ignorance"—the obscuring views that prevent us from seeing things as they truly are.

This profoundly uplifting, creative revelation of the spiritual nature of being human—contrary to common sense, counterintuitive to our usual way of viewing the world—is encouraging and inspiring. Yet just hearing or talking about our inherently enlightened nature is not enough to understand its deepest meaning. And how easy it is to slide into sarcasm or criticism when reflecting on the foolish behavior of humanity. If we are not careful, the cynicism can become a habit.

Buddhism and Zen emphasize meditation practice as the effective way to appreciate our own true nature and that of others. Because we are foolish creatures and quick to judge, we are at risk for failing to understand our fundamental spiritual nature, to know that we are already bodhisattvas, inherently wise and inherently compassionate.

If someone cuts me off in traffic and I become upset, I have the choice of letting go of my emotion by recognizing that he is simply being foolish. But if I allow myself to take it personally, to indulge my momentary anger and want to get even, I may, through my own foolish action, create a dangerous situation that could lead to suffering for me and for others.

The spiritual practice of meditation, however, can begin to open up other options.

THE ROUGH EDGES OF ANGER

What trances of torture does that man endure who is consumed with one unachieved revengeful desire. He sleeps with clenched hands; and wakes with his own bloody nails in his palms.

—*Herman Melville*

Several months after starting Zen practice, more than forty years ago, I realized how I continued to be troubled by aspects of myself I didn't like. I had expected they would be somehow magically dissolved by meditation—and in a very short time! Yet they persisted. I brought my concern to one of the Zen teachers who had come from Japan to help establish Zen in America. "My anger," I told him, "it just doesn't go away!" He smiled, surprisingly nonchalant about my dismay. "Oh," he said, "that's just some rough edges." His remark was a revelation and a relief. From it, I understood that my seeming "impurity" was not a major defect, my anger was simply something to take care of. Inherently, there was nothing wrong with me.

Nonetheless, anger can be a real source of suffering. Second only to natural disasters, anger is the greatest destroyer of individuals, personal relationships, and entire societies. Early psychological theories of aggression led to the belief that anger should be expressed, that we should "get it all out." Modern science (and much of our own actual experience, I suspect) shows that simply expressing anger turns out not to be helpful; in fact, acting from anger increases the anger as well as its negative physiological impact on our bodies and minds.

Anger arises in us as a result of something someone did or said—and often, that someone is us ourselves. The word or deed touches a sensitive place in our psyche, breaching our refuge. Anger may be the tip of our emotional iceberg, because we often harbor underlying feelings that, when aroused, create the anger. These can include embarrassment, fear, guilt, insecurity, rejection, or humiliation. Becoming aware of our anger is a good thing. It provides an opportunity to reflect and recognize the deeper feeling that, when explored and understood—without the necessity of being entirely resolved—will lead to emotional relief and a greater sense of freedom. Awareness of anger is vital: by not facing and resolving it in a timely manner, it can develop into a grudge. If left unchecked, it evolves further into a desire for personal revenge, to punish the other person who *seems* to have made us feel so bad.

Anger and its corollaries have a blinding effect on our capacities to reason and relate, short-circuiting our potential to be resourceful in difficult or uncomfortable situations. Yet once we recognize and accept that anger has arisen we can let it go by understanding that the feeling arose in us because of something someone did or said and that despite our imagined justification, there is no real need for us to take any of it personally.

When examined carefully, especially through the lens of meditation practice, we can come to see that this arisen feeling of burning rage in fact has neither substance nor permanency; it is, in this sense, weightless, or, in Buddhist parlance, *empty*. But anger becomes a heavy, lingering, emotional burden when we continue to carry around what someone says or does, needlessly creating a weight in our mind. Awareness of our self in a given situation can show us that the action of the other person, no matter how painful we feel because of it, is very likely a mistake on their part, based on foolishness, misunderstanding, or that person's own burdensome suffering.

And that very recognition can often relieve us of the need to take it personally, leaving anger no place to reside.

THE COMPLAINER

It is like a blue flower blooming in the tropical heat. If you experience tropical heat surely you will experience the blue lotus.
—Zen Master Dogen

Human history is the record of the key events, individuals, and social forces that contour civilizations and create new forms of societies. Yet history is more than incidents and personalities; it chronicles the difficulties of being human, as it traces our struggles to find meaning in life against the odds of injustice and bad luck. In this regard, all of history is a study of human suffering and mankind's efforts to end it. But the study of history alone cannot show us how to end suffering.

We can only begin that process by understanding suffering's true source, starting by examining the stories of life, in fine detail, through the microscope of observation, discernment, and thoughtfulness. Watching carefully the moment-by-moment unfolding story of our own life is the emphasis of meditative spiritual practice. Bringing these same dispositions to the stories of others—including those created by master storytellers—we can be enlightened by lives other than our own.

In *The Adventures of Augie March,* a classic of early twentieth-century America, Nobel Laureate Saul Bellow creates a modern Odyssey describing how people create suffering for both themselves and others out of their own desperate search for recognition and satisfaction. Augie is a poor boy growing up in Depression-era Chicago. His family is ruled by Grandma, who aspires to train him in the ways of getting by and doing well in the world, of rising above present circumstances. Her methods are harsh: she punishes, threatens, criticizes, and demeans. She never listens, nor shows outward affection or feelings, except disdain. To shape and strengthen him she admonishes Augie to withhold love, telling him: "Nobody asks you to love the whole world…the more you love people, the more they'll mix you up. A child loves, a person respects. Respect is better than love."

Grandma's advice reflects the popular wisdom, a safe—if isolating—commonsense philosophy for pursuing personal success. But if we want to live in harmony with each other, we shouldn't believe it; we mustn't fall for Grandma's line, a view that comes from misunderstanding and denial. Grandma tragically sees so many of us as inherently unlovable; we can after all be selfish, arrogant, sloppy, foolish, and stubborn. Who could care for such difficult people? And who would want to make the effort to understand them? It's so often easier to be the complainer: to disdain and grouse about others and write them off, to remain thoroughly self-oriented.

Yet the truth is that love is our natural state. Not the popular notion of love—obsessive attraction and devotion to one person, but a more intrinsic, selfless quality of caring that is the bright mark of humanity at its finest. This love is a concern for the well-being of others, a willingness to be honest, generous, patient, responsible, helpful—and forgiving. It is characterized by equanimity, and acceptance, extending to everyone, independent of who they are, how they behave, or whether they meet some arbitrary criteria of being how we think they should be.

It is easy to fall into the trap of cynicism and complaint, to believe what Augie's Grandma believes. But Grandma is small-minded, sadly incapable of seeing other people as anything other than a collection of annoying faults. As Augie describes her, "Her memory specialized in (other's) misdemeanors and offenses, which were as ineradicable from her brain as the patrician wrinkle was between her eyes, and her dissatisfaction was an element and a part of nature."

So, how then can we come to see otherwise, to see people as lovable? Only by recognizing their—and our—inherent perfection and by understanding how a harsh life can make harsh people. Bellow speaks through Augie: "Before vice and shortcomings, admitted in the weariness of maturity, ...there are, or supposed to be, silken, unconscious, nature-painted times, like the pastoral of Sicilian shepherd lovers.... But when there is no shepherd-Sicily, no freehand nature-painting, but deep city vexation instead, and you are forced into deep city aims...what can that lead to of the highest?"

How do we escape the trap, see the natural state? We must learn to cultivate selflessness—the only freedom there is from the small-minded prison of our own self-importance—accompanied by understanding. Selfless and understanding: to cultivate one is to cultivate the other. The cultivation of selflessness arises out of the quiet discipline of a spiritual practice like meditation.

Such a practice enlarges our understanding of how we needlessly create problems, and opens the way for us to nurture a generous spirit in all relationships. It opens the way for us to be something other than the complainer. The pull toward spiritual practice always comes, on some level, from a sense that universal love is natural, that it can should be lived and expressed. Perhaps this it what Augie senses when he expresses what so many of us have felt, "I know I longed very much but I didn't know for what."

STRESS AND STRESS PREVENTION

Nobody sees any one as he is—they see all sorts of things—they see themselves...
—*Virginia Woolf*

We may dream and fantasize of being free of stress but such a state is not possible. Stress is a part of the very business of life. The reason is simple: stress is a result of relationships with things and with people. And, since nothing in life is fixed, all things and relationships inevitably change—and a disturbed, formerly stable relationship creates stress. We cannot avoid coming face to face with stress and indeed much of our life is about how we relate to changes.

Usually, we think of stress as something personal, as our own. We may wonder, "How can I relieve my stress?" But when we recognize that stress is a result of a change in a relationship—involving self and other, not just self—we appreciate how our well-being is best served when our highest priority is the creation and maintenance of healthy relationships. Understanding this point, we are careful to avoid allowing a change in a mutually beneficial relationship—one with a common objective—to create a broken relationship. Our guideline is necessarily "stay connected."

Stress has a peculiar quality: it doesn't get better if we try to make it "go away." That approach to stress only creates separation in the relationship. For example, if I am driving to work and my car suddenly stops for no apparent reason, it does no good to abandon the car on the freeway with a feeling of, "I don't have to deal with you!" I may experience immediate, temporary relief by walking away from the suddenly stressful situation, but I have not solved the problem in the long run. I have succeeded only in creating additional stress. Many of our relationships with things and people can be just like this.

Life continually presents situations that we would love to make "go away." The temptation can be great. A coworker says or does something that offends or irritates, initiating the urge to turn your back on him and walk away. Another email arrives in the long queue: you consider the DELETE button with a sense of frustration. The mailman delivers a letter from the IRS informing you that your tax return contains an error, not in your favor: the wastebasket beckons. The secretary of an important client calls to tell you that today's meeting—that took you months to arrange—is canceled because "something came up." You acknowledge politely, avoiding the urge to slam down the telephone and cross the offending person off your list. In each of these situations, "avoiding the hassle" is not creative: it only leads to future problems and potentially greater stress.

Trying to achieve and remain in what we imagine to be a stress-free zone is an unrealistic goal. Instead, it is more important to increase our capacity to respond to stress in a positive way, not only for our self but for others in our life. In order to avoid responding in harmful ways, we need to be aware of our sudden urges and of our old, habitual, uncreative ways of reacting to difficult situations.

Enhancing our skill of awareness increases our capacity to perceive when a change may be starting to take place in a relationship, and this awareness enhances our ability to respond skillfully, creatively. Early recognition prevents us from being surprised later when the change has grown so large that it threatens the relationship altogether. It also enables us to act in ways that help the relationship evolve smoothly into a new form, if the conditions that are causing the change truly are inevitable. Meditation practice fosters this kind of awareness. In addition, meditation practice increases our capacity to be consciously aware that we are, indeed, *feeling stressed.*

Rather than simply having an ambiguous, nagging feeling, the awareness signals that we have a challenge that needs addressing. Although it may seem counter-intuitive, awareness of our stress can be helpful—in the recognition of a problem, followed by the exploration of the problem, and finally in developing a strategy or plan for resolving the problem. If we can avoid falling into the trap of trying to "make it go away," awareness of stress is the positive first step in resolving the stressful situation.

Zazen, Zen meditation, is not a stress reduction technique, such as massage, exercise, sitting in a hot tub, or vacationing in Hawaii. Those activities can relieve the physical and emotional symptoms of stress but they do not get to its source. If you have a massage at 10:30 in the morning, you will probably need another at 3:00 in the afternoon. If you go to Hawaii for two weeks, you will feel refreshed and ready to go when you return, but a week later, you will need another vacation. Stress reduction techniques will relax us, but they do not increase our capacity to respond positively to stressful situations. The aware-ness practice of zazen enhances that capacity, enabling us to perceive and resolve the stressful feeling before it becomes overwhelming. In that way, zazen—as an ongoing rather than occasional practice—is a stress-*prevention* activity, enabling our mind to quickly regain calmness when a stress-inducing situation arises. It increases our capacity to go home from work at the end of the day feeling buoyant, rather than wiped out. Instead of worrying about the stressful situations waiting for us tomorrow, we have the confidence that we will be able to respond to them in a positive way.

THE "I HAVE TO" TRAP

*Like a tiny drop of dew, or a bubble floating
in a stream; like a flash of lightning in a
summer cloud, or a flickering lamp, an
illusion, a phantom, or a dream.*

—*The Buddha*

*All that we see or seem
Is but a dream within a dream.*

—*Edgar Allen Poe*

A musician understands the critical need to pay attention, to maintain awareness of hands, feet, mouth, instrument, sounds, and the other musicians. To create music, his mind must be focused; to allow it to wander leads to noise. The same is true for even the most mundane activities of daily life. However, distracting thoughts flow like an endless river. And like the river, they exert a powerful pull that can dislodge awareness from what we do.

During meditation, we experience the intrusive power of thoughts generated by the mind. And it doesn't actually help to pit our will against them, trying to create a wall to keep them out. Just the opposite occurs: we become more stubborn and create even more emotion and anxiety when we defend against them. In Zen practice, we don't try to "cut off" thoughts. We simply notice when they appear, momentarily acknowledge them with the same attitude we would an old friend, and let them go by not attaching our attention to them.

Letting go has two stages, beginning with recognition of the potentially distracting thought temporarily claiming the spotlight. This is followed by taking back the spotlight, by keeping the mind's attention where it is, returning it to where we'd like it to be. The first part requires awareness. The second needs our determination not to be tempted to stray from the present moment.

It is difficult to imagine anyone in this busy world who has not been bothered by the sudden feeling, "I have to go do *something* (other than what I am presently doing)." If the intruding thought has a great deal of energy and does not fade away, it is very likely accompanied by anxiety or tension. Its persistence and our stress are the banners of our old nemesis, the "I Have To" trap.

To escape the trap, it is necessary to consciously examine the urge to do something else; the notion may or may not be valid. Its validity is based on the priorities of the present situation as well as our own personal criteria for making decisions, our own sense of urgency. Escaping the trap is a three-step process: recognizing and acknowledging the feeling, determining if it is valid according to the situation, and deciding what to do. We have two choices for the last step: either shift the spotlight or leave it where it is. If the intruding idea truly must be addressed now, if we need to turn it into the new current task—then we must reschedule the task we have been working on and give our attention to the new. Otherwise, if our belief that we "have to" do something else right now is not valid, we can then continue with our present task and make a note to take care of the new idea later.

If we don't get to step three—the critical point of having a choice and making a decision—we may stay stuck in the "I Have To" trap with its relentless message, "I must, I must, I must!" The continuous pressure of "I Have To..." is where stress begins. Staying stuck without a decision, there is no relief from the pressure.

STAYING STUCK

*When an opportunity comes do not let it pass
by, yet always think twice before acting.*

        —*Soyen Shaku*

Discouragement damages our sense of well-being. It can become dangerous if not resolved, growing into depression, expanding into a large, pervasive hopelessness about life. Understanding discouragement's true source—not just its *apparent* source—and being prepared to respond positively to the conditions that create it, enables us to minimize the helpless feeling and subtle anxiety that accompany it.

Overemphasis on achievement and success is now a fundamental source of discouragement in our competitive society. The results-oriented culture demands successful "payoffs" from even the most routine daily activities. If we are not careful, our scorecard of "payoffs"—how well and how often we attain the payoffs we think we want—becomes an artificial measure of our personal value, as if each of us were a marketable commodity. Such a statistic is more than misleading: in no way does it reveal the true value of an individual life. And it is also dangerous: the appeal of its bottom-line neatness can lure us into a simplistic, thoughtless worldview of humanity.

Caught up in the belief that successful "payoffs" are the primary purpose of life's activities, we fill our mind with expectations. Even if we have the good fortune to meet most of them, we can never meet all of our expectations. As a result, disappointment becomes a frequent visitor. But disappointment, though painful, is not an inherently damaging experience; a great deal can be learned from an activity that does not turn out as we might hope. We use what we learn from the effort—in the laboratory, the office, the studio, the classroom, the kitchen, the conference room, or at home plate—in our next try, and in this very moment as well. Our challenge is to prevent disappointment—a single moment event—from turning into discouragement, a dark, cave-like state of mind that lingers over time.

Like a boat adrift in horse latitudes, discouragement develops when the mind dwells on past disappointments. Whether these disappointments result from our own carelessness, from a failed trial-and-error experiment conducted in search of knowledge, from a decision that missed the mark because sufficient information and time were not available to support our judgment, or from losing a competitive game, the state of "dwelling" is the enemy. Staying stuck in the past, failing to move on, severely inhibits the mind from paying attention to what is going on in the present moment.

The best response is heightened awareness. Surprisingly, recognition of a growing or lingering sense of discouragement is helpful, alerting us that the mind has become distracted by feelings of past disappointments. The awareness is truly a wake up call; we are fortunate when it occurs. It provides us the opportunity to make a conscious effort to bring our attention back to the task, or relationship, at hand. It lets us know that we have been carrying around something in our mind, affecting our attitude toward our work, or what we have to do. And it is a signal that we may have established expectations for activities that do not require them, or should not have them.

Continually enhancing our awareness skill diminishes the danger of drifting into discouragement. It prevents the inevitable disappointments from piling up, from becoming an anchor. Our increased capacity to let go of disappointment is one of the major practical benefits of zazen.

Beginning to see the potential of feeling upbeat in the midst of disappointment is the surest sign that our practice is going well.

THE WALL

To set up what you like against what you dislike is the disease of the mind.

—Zen Master Sengcan

Like anger, resistance robs the mind of creativity. It arises when we feel we either do not want or are not able to give our full attention to a task, a problem, or a personal relationship. It is different from a conscious, objectively reasoned decision to choose not to do something. Rather, resistance is an aversion—an invisible wall—turning us away from a place we prefer not to go.

The turning away is usually the result of other feelings. Perhaps our unconscious avoidance is a result of fear—of failure, of embarrassment, of being bored, of not being appreciated. Perhaps we resist speaking to an old friend or relative because we are angry at something she said months ago. Or maybe we feel that an activity is unimportant and not worth the effort, not appreciating that someone else is waiting for us to act or respond.

The greater our capacity of awareness, the greater our chances of recognizing resistance when it arises. Then we have the opportunity to take a deep breath and acknowledge the resistance, and perhaps explore the underlying feeling. Our nonjudgmental awareness avoids resistance, enabling us to give full attention to what we have to do.

On the other hand, if we judge an activity according to our personal preferences—whether we care for it or not—we are likely to put it off or avoid it altogether, running the risk of creating a problem for ourselves down the road. More creative and more satisfying in the long run is to make a conscious decision to do or not do something by thinking through the pros and cons of the activity itself, without judging it according to our own desires.

THE EMPEROR'S CLOTHES

*When I was a child, I spake as a child, I felt as
a child, I thought as a child: now that I am
become a man, I have put away childish
things.*

—*I Corinthians 13:11*

Bodhidharma is one of the most familiar and
popular figures in Zen literature. He is said to
be the twenty-eight patriarch of Buddhism in
India, credited with bringing Zen to China in the sixth
century. Although scholars debate the historical accuracy of his life, his legend is studied and discussed
with great interest.

There is famous koan, a Zen teaching story, about
Bodhidharma's conversation with Emperor Wu. The
emperor was a devout patron of Buddhism. He
actively studied the scriptures, financed the building
of temples, and provided support for the monks.

According to the legend, soon after Bodhidharma arrived in China, the emperor summoned him for an audience.

The emperor asked, "I have devoted my wealth and my administration to bring Buddhism to this country. I have built many monasteries, had sutras copied, and had images made. How much merit have I earned?"

Bodhidharma answered, "No merit."

The emperor was surprised by this answer and asked further: "So then what is the highest meaning of the holy teaching?"

Bodhidharma answered, "No holiness, emptiness."

The emperor then asked, "Who are you?"

Bodhidharma responded, "I don't know."

Bodhidharma then left the palace and went to another part of the country.

Later, the emperor asked his minister about the encounter. The minister in turn asked the emperor if he knew who Bodhidharma really was. The emperor did not, so the official explained that Bodhidharma was the manifestation of the Bodhisattva Kwan Yin, bringing Buddha's teaching. The emperor regretted his behavior toward Bodhidharma and wanted to bring him back. The official said it wasn't possible, he would not come back.

Through the enigmatic behavior of Bodhidharma, this *koan* expresses the fundamental teachings of Zen. At the same time, it demonstrates humanity's tragic flaw in the way the emperor relates to the wise and renowned Buddhist master in front of him. The emperor appears to be an unselfish supporter of Buddhism, yet his questioning illustrates his concern for personal gain. At one level, he is hoping to acquire "merit," which, as taught in early Buddhism, would enable him to gain a favorable next life, even *Nirvana* (heaven). So his efforts in establishing Buddhism—as helpful as they may be to the general population— have in reality been an investment in his own salvation. Impressed with himself, he has not been as charitable as he believes himself to be: he is looking for a payoff. By his response—*No merit*—Bodhidharma is signaling that the emperor does not understand Buddhism, misunderstands its spirit.

At another level, the emperor is fishing for acknowledgment and praise from the renowned teacher. He is disappointed: Bodhidharma is firm and unwavering, refusing to give the emperor the expected admiration, refusing to encourage misunderstanding. A strict teacher, disdaining politeness for truth, Bodhidharma remains the model of authenticity. Not receiving the admiration he craves, the emperor reacts with annoyance and impatience. The opportunity for understanding is lost.

The emperor believes he is a good Buddhist, but he has been merely a poster Buddhist. His tragedy is his delusive belief in gain and admiration as meaningful goals to be pursued. His actions—oriented toward his own self-interests—may seem charitable yet they have not brought personal salvation. However, learning from his disappointment, his regret may signal a turn of mind.

This koan demonstrates how we can be either like the emperor, orienting our life toward our own personal gain—creating an image and playing a role in order to gain admiration and praise, like a child—or like Bodhidharma, cutting through delusion and living authentically, just simply being who we are, without imitation.

MIND SHADOWS

Men cannot remain content with what is given them by their culture if they are to be fully human.

—*Allan Bloom*

n "The Myth of the Cave," Plato provides a thoughtful as well as disturbing portrayal of how the thinking mind relates to the phenomenal world. In his allegory, he depicts humans as prisoners, forced to look at shadows on the wall of the cave, seeing merely projected images of things of the world. Mankind, Plato tells us, accepts the shadows as the things themselves, as reality itself. For him, freedom requires that we leave the cave, to go where light illuminates the true nature of things. His story contends that the human mind is easily deceived, but that it is possible for us to become free of confusion by expanding our capacity to reason, that thoughtful people can find truth by shining the light of inquiry on shadowy images.

Later Western philosophers of the seventeenth and eighteenth centuries believed that all men could be enlightened by expanding their capacity to reason. Their premise: intellectual training opens the mind to see beyond its limited, biased views. But in this view, something vital is overlooked. The emphasis on the power of logic and rational thinking does not account for emotional tendencies that get in the way of our ability to see things as they are. Fear, desire, and ambition conspire to convince the mind that it needs to delude itself to protect its flattering, defensive self-image. In situations that threaten the ego, reason is at risk of being carried away by emotions and the self-deceptions they create.

Seven centuries after Plato, half a world beyond Greece, the legendary Bodhidharma is reported to have sat in meditation for nine years, facing the wall of his cave in northeastern China, following his meeting with Emperor Wu. Bodhidharma was not a prisoner; he was there by choice. For him, meditation practice was the expression of inherent freedom. In this allegory, he willingly enters the cave of his mind to face his delusions clearly and thereby express his freedom from them.

Bodhidharma's cave—the place of enlightenment, the metaphor of his continuous spiritual practice—is the opposite of Plato's. For Plato, the cave is the place of *un*enlightenment, a place to escape. Both caves are places where delusions appear, so in that sense they are similar. However, Bodhidharma understands delusions, the way they distort understanding and interfere with clear perception.

To be honest in everyday life is not always easy when we are in Plato's cave. Yet, when we are part of a society that values honesty, there is help for us in the form of parental guidance, religious education, and social norms. On the other hand, to be honest in our own mind is a greater challenge, as delusions appear over and over again—and we are on our own to make this discovery and confront them.

We have all seen how even highly intelligent people can make poor decisions or act irrationally or selfishly when distracted and fooled by misleading, projected images. No one can watch our thoughts and feelings for us, no one can train us from the outside—not parents, church, school, or society. We have to train ourselves; we have to leave Plato's cave and have the courage to enter Bodhidharma's.

Our attitude determines what cave we live in, how we choose to see the world. To be honest in our own mind, to be free of the delusions that create shadows, we have to continually empty our mind of the made-up stories we tell ourselves. And if we feel strongly about the need for such honesty—if we recognize how easily we fool ourselves—we will readily enter the spiritual practice that enables us to avoid the strong undertow of self-deceit. We have to enter Bodhidharma's cave so that we can see delusions for what they are—shadows on the wall—and not be fooled by them.

If we simply assume that our own mind is free of delusions, or if we rationalize them away, we are choosing Plato's cave, falling into the trap of relying on intellect and reason to show us the truth. But logic and reason alone cannot bring enlightenment to the mind as Plato promised: we cannot pursue reason without distortion if we are convinced that the very act of pursuing reason is itself inherently "pure," untouched by ego, by subjective intention.

Acknowledging the difficulty of being honest because of our human tendency for self deceit, we must return to Bodhidharma's cave. We need spiritual practice, not just philosophy, to live the enlightened life.

STAGNATION

*Then I looked on all the works that my hands
had wrought and on the labor that I had
labored to do; and, behold, all was vanity and
a striving after wind, and there was no profit
under the sun.*

—Ecclesiastes 2:11

In an ancient parable, a man dies and finds himself
in a very beautiful place. He is greeted by a gracious attendant who tells the man he can have
anything he wants. Every comfort, food, physical
pleasure, excitement, and entertainment is available
to him at any time. The man is delighted. For days, he
indulges all of his senses in pleasure, enjoying the
familiar as well as the new. But after a time, he
becomes bored, uninspired, with nothing to look forward to. He asks his helpful attendant for some work
but is told that there is no such thing as work where

he is now. The man says, "No work! I may just as well be in hell!" The attendant replies, "Where do you think you are?"

This is a story of what becomes of a mind that remains attached to the pursuit of pleasure and comfort. It is an illustration of the need to engage in meaningful activity that makes a life fulfilling, connected, rather than just going through the motions. Without this attitude, we are told, our life stagnates—and we are in hell.

The most important tenet of the contemplative schools of Buddhism declares that everyone, without exception, is inherently enlightened, that each of us has access to the same compassion and wisdom that the Buddha found—but that without spiritual practice, this potential remains dormant. It is why Buddhists put emphasis on meditation practice that suspends self-gratification in favor of a mind continually ready for selfless response to whatever situation life brings, of a mind that does not stagnate. This emphasis includes continuous practice, not just when convenient or when feeling stress, in the understanding that without continuity of spiritual expression, life becomes stagnant.

Although meditation practice has gained increasing acceptance in recent years, it is still not easy for most people to accept the idea that continuous spiritual practice is vital for an authentic life: we are ingrained with the belief that we are entitled to all the comforts and conveniences our culture has to offer. A few years ago, I spoke with a group of students at a local university about my experiences of the ways Zen practice influenced my life. One of the young men was skeptical of the whole idea. "My spiritual practice is golf; I don't need to do meditation," was his argument. From his standpoint, any activity that gives pleasure and relaxation—eating, drinking, sex, music, television, sports—can be construed as "spiritual practice." Our clever human mind can rationalize its way into believing anything it wants, into ignoring anything that appears to attack its self-interests.

Before we can work with the stuff of daily life, we have to learn how to *work* in its larger sense. It means doing what we have to do without being distracted by preconceived ideas of comfort and pleasure. If we feel that we are in hell but are unwilling to practice—to get to work—we will feel as if we are live bait, no more than a worm on the hook of self-satisfaction, stuck in one place, squirming to get free.

The awareness of feeling that we are in hell—that our life is not flowing—is as much an opportunity as it is a problem. The pain of the feeling is a wake-up call, a chance to explore our life, to understand our self, and to see the reason behind our suffering. However, if we deny the feeling, if we are unwilling to do the work of spiritual practice, we will find that there is "no work" and will remain in hell. Acknowledging our hell-bound feeling is the starting point for understanding that we are caught up in attachments and preconceived ideas. To get off the hook, it is necessary to engage in spiritual practice with a sense of determination, to engage in the real work of life.

The story of our man who mistakenly believed he had arrived at heaven parallels the story of Buddha. In that legend, after thirty years of privilege and luxury behind palace walls, the young prince who is to become Buddha desires to know what the everyday world is like. What he sees of human suffering inspires him to leave the royal life, to enter the world of ordinary people, and to find some way to help, some way to serve others. Becoming sick from overdosing on pleasure, he seeks engagement, which becomes both his work and his spiritual practice.

CARRIED AWAY

Five senses; an incurably abstract intellect;
a haphazardly selective memory; a set of
preconceptions and assumptions so numerous
that I can never examine more than a minority
of them—never become conscious of them all.
How much of total Reality can such an
apparatus let through?

—*C.S. Lewis*

I n business schools throughout the land, bright and energetic men and women endure challenging academic programs, expanding their professional options and improving their chances for success and satisfaction in their careers. With the help of case studies and computer simulations, they sharpen their decision-making and problem-solving skills. They emerge richer in knowledge, and with greater creative potential.

Yet there is a prerequisite for fulfilling that potential and exercising that knowledge in real-life situations. For without the capacity of *awareness*—having a mind undistracted by uninvited, extraneous ideas that seem to carry a sense of urgency or by feelings that short circuit the intellectual process—critical thinking and creativity are diminished.

The gifts of our individual experience, intellect, and training set the stage for creative responses to the full range of human opportunities, problems, and choices, from those that influence entire societies to what to order for lunch. But even when our endowments are abundant, two phenomena get in the way of creating a helpful and productive decision or solution: the assumptions we make about a situation and the biases and emotions that we carry in the back of our mind. Decisions and solutions are at risk of being flawed—making them potentially dangerous—when we are not cognizant of our assumptions—leaving them unexamined, or when we are unaware of hidden feelings, moods, or passions, making them all the more powerful.

Zen practice puts great emphasis on keeping an open mind, not hindered by personal bias of likes and dislikes and of the emotions that often accompany them, as reflected in the ancient saying:

The Great Way isn't difficult
For those who are unattached to their
preferences.
Let go of longing and aversion,
And everything will be perfectly clear.

The reality of daily life requires us to judge, to make choices, to accept or reject elements of situations that appear before us. How can we accomplish that responsibility without becoming carried away by personal preferences?

The awareness-enhancing nature of zazen practice increases our chances of recognizing our own mental process, enabling us to perceive and acknowledge our emotions and preconceived ideas. This recognition provides the opportunity to examine these potential blocks to creativity so that we can think things through. Unbiased critical thinking shines the light of intellect on many dimensions of the situation we face: its details and complexity, its place in the "big picture"—that is, its relationship to other situations and individuals—the pros and cons of actions we may take, and, perhaps most important, an insight into potential unintended consequences of our action or inaction.

Awareness of our feelings and attachments to old ways of doing things helps us separate them from the actual problem at hand. And when we can do that we have a chance to address a difficult situation without being distracted by our own emotional needs, fulfilling a second prerequisite for resolving a problem creatively: the desire for a solution that will be of benefit to others.

NO PROMISES

A certain amount of care or pain or trouble is necessary for every man at all times.

—*Arthur Schopenhauer*

In zazen, making our best effort to remain still, we become aware of small discomforts that we normally brush away without thinking during daily life: the itch on the nose, the fly buzzing around our ear, the foot falling asleep, the small ache in our back. Discomfort, the uninvited guest whose presence threatens to break up our party, inevitably shows up during quiet meditation. It arrives unannounced, but soon makes its presence known, dressed in any number of different attires, from a minor annoyance to angst to various degrees of pain. The way we respond to the intrusion is vital.

The first question of many beginning Zen practitioners concerns the intruding discomfort: "When does it go away?" The easy answer is, of course, a variation of, "It's hard to say." But the most realistic answer is, "Maybe it doesn't." This comes as a shock and a disappointment. "Isn't it *supposed to* get easier?" they ask. Again the answer must necessarily be unsatisfying: "Try not to be concerned with what is *supposed to* happen. Simply allow your mind to rest in the present." So the first quality of mind that we notice when we begin meditation practice is anxiety for the discomfort that quietly takes us by surprise. When it does come up, we immediately seek for some assurance, a promise, that it will go away. But spiritual practice dissipates with reliance on promises; we have to be a bit tough-minded and let them go. Practice is about the effort we make in whatever situation arises in life. It discourages clinging to the "good stuff" and pushing away the "bad stuff." Rather, spiritual practice encourages us to drop off the habit of clinging and pushing away. It emphasizes our attitude and approach to the current activity, avoiding the distraction of foggy future promises.

Logically, we may think, "If I meditate long enough, eventually there will be no more pain when I sit." But this idea is a misunderstanding of spiritual practice. It is the same kind of thinking that says, "When I have attained what I want, I won't need to practice any more." This attitude does not lead to the relief of anxiety. Instead, it actually becomes yet another *source* of anxiety.

Our attitude toward physical discomfort during meditation should be to let it appear when it appears, trying not to treat it as "the enemy." In other words, we try not to fight it off or wish that it would go away. We simply accept it because it is what is happening in the present moment. The point is not to let physical discomfort become emotional pain. The mind that frets about discomfort in the knee or in the back does so from personal self-concern. To hold the idea "I don't like this discomfort! I want it to go away" is how the mind creates suffering for itself. But when it lets go of the desire for comfort, the mind feels no pain.

It is natural to be distracted by physical or emotional discomfort when we first start to practice zazen. It wasn't expected; we don't know what to do about it. And so we naturally struggle to find some way to make it vanish. But actually, experiencing discomfort can help our practice because *it gets our attention*. The physical sensation brings the wandering mind back to the reality of the present moment and helps it understand how easily it can be distracted by desires. If we worry about the feeling of discomfort, it is just the ego pleading, "I deserve comfort!" So we try not to worry about the pain in our legs.

This attitude does not mean that we need ignore a physical discomfort that is becoming a debilitating pain. It is not necessary to turn meditation into an ascetic practice; torture is not the point. The point is to become aware of our desires, to recognize when our concern about our discomfort is really a disguised concern for loss of comfort or if we really do need to take an easier posture. Each of us has to make this personal determination.

The best way to take care of pain is with a soft, flexible mind, a "big mind" that includes everything. It is the mind that always looks straight ahead, that is not distracted by desire on the left or discomfort on the right. When discomfort does arise, the important point is to refrain from immediately adjusting the posture. Instead, we focus attention on the place of discomfort, acknowledge it, accept it, without trying to push it or force it away. We treat it as if it were a guest. We see if you can sit quietly for another ten seconds without scratching the itch, brushing away the mosquito, or shifting the leg. Then we try another ten seconds. In other words, we don't declare war on the discomfort as if it were an invader. When we do become aware of pain or discomfort, a gracious, non-combative attitude expands our "comfort zone" and helps increase our tolerance for uninvited irritations. Consider how this aware, patient, and accepting attitude toward discomfort might express itself in personal relations in difficult work situations and in other areas of life.

COMPLICATING OUR LIFE

*Wise indeed is the man who contemplates
the nature, arising, and cessation of passion—
and knows that it only leads to sorrow.*

—*The Buddha*

Quiet laughter flowed from the bar in the early evening. The atmosphere was warm, the service courteous in the dark wood and leather midtown Manhattan steak house. I was down from college visiting my father for the weekend, as I did whenever we could both manage it during the school year. My dad was a gregarious, successful businessman with many friends who shared his interest in sporting events, gin-rummy, good food, and single-malt scotch. They enjoyed their work and their lives. They were upbeat and jovial, full of man-talk and of themselves. I was looking forward to being with them.

One of my father's friends was a well-known Seventh Avenue manufacturer of women's fashion clothing. He was smart, generous, and fun-loving. I liked him. He always made it a point to be friendly: "How you doing, kid. How's school? How's the football team?" He was married, with two young daughters. He also had two girlfriends, as was well-known.

After drinks, during the main course, my father's friend leaned over to him. His expression had changed, the smile was gone. With averted eyes and a hushed voice he said to my father, "Larry, how can I simplify my life?" My father shook his head slightly and with a barely noticeable wave of his hand indicated, "Not now." I was startled by my dad's friend's question. I pictured him worldly and wise, on top of his life, in control. The naive college kid was confused.

Driving back to school that Sunday, I thought about the previous evening. Several hours behind the wheel gave me a chance to reflect on what I heard and saw. I didn't comprehend why my dad's friend was troubled. Years later, I came to understand something about how we make problems for ourselves.

Our mind is continually distracted by notions of excitement, success, affirmation, and entertainment. All have great appeal; we anticipate their taste. Unfortunately, pursuing them robs the mind of clarity and equanimity; our perspective becomes fogged, like a windshield on a misty night. We fail to recognize that we are making our life more complex with activities of pursuit. I'm sure that's what happened to my father's friend.

Too often our mind does not recognize that our everyday "doing" is oriented toward "pursuing." And this lack of recognition is how pride, fear, the quest for fame, and the need to "win" are added to what we do. When we mix in such ingredients, our activity does not feel right; we are unsatisfied by what we are doing, even though we may be judged to be successful in everyday affairs. The sense of dissatisfaction may itself be subtle; we have no understanding of where it comes from or how to get rid of it. This nagging feeling is one reason we turn to spiritual practice.

In our endeavors to lead satisfying lives, we try to be successful in what we do. But if pursuit of success and its corollary—conquest—is the main point of our effort, we are in danger of complicating our lives, of misplacing the subtlety of mind, and losing sight of Reality. Success can be intoxicating; we get high on the excitement it brings. Yet, what we truly want more than success is to understand the meaning of our life and how to live in a fulfilling way in a complex world. Too much concern for success erodes our mind's flexibility and subtleness, and prevents us from appreciating life and its meaning.

THE PRACTICE

THE SKILL OF AWARENESS

This life of ours would not cause you sorrow
if you thought of it as like
the mountain cherry blossoms
which bloom and fade in a day.

—*Lady Murasaki Shikibu*

There's an old Zen story about a government official who went to visit a well-known Zen master:

"Times are difficult and the people suffer. I am responsible for their well-being and am at a loss how to help them. Please instruct me."

The Zen master picked up his brush, dipped it in ink, and wrote the Chinese character that means ATTENTION.

The official became angry: "I come for your help to relieve suffering and you give me just a single word! I ask again for the wisdom to help others."
The master then wrote two more characters:

ATTENTION

ATTENTION

Cancer patients are now practicing meditation, as are pregnant women, people with chronic pain, and individuals who want to learn how to forgive. In addition to its medical and emotional benefits, meditation improves the quality of life by enhancing awareness, which is our most important skill. All of the useful skills and talents that we develop during our lifetime depend on the level of awareness we bring to each moment, to each activity. Awareness is the basis for the capacity to listen attentively, feel deeply, and read with comprehension. Attention also helps us, for instance, to write with clarity and to verbally express ideas fully and with accuracy. Of most importance, awareness enables us to respond creatively and positively to all the complex situations that arise in our life.

For whatever reason people are drawn to meditation—as a spiritual practice, to improve health, to be more in touch with daily life, or simply as a way to relax—they have discovered that it is fundamentally the practice of awareness, whether on the meditation cushion, at work, or at home. It creates an opportunity for the mind to find balance and calmness by limiting activities, both mental and physical. The mind can accept the opportunity by giving itself permission to set aside its problem-solving and intellectual activity for a short time, to do "nothing" other than make an effort to keep attention on the present moment. Meditation then becomes the antidote to distractions, the remedy for the stress of "multitasking."

The first time people try meditation, they quickly discover the difficulty of maintaining awareness of their breath. The discovery unmasks "the enemy," the human mind's tendency to become distracted by fantasy; by feelings of excitement—as well as of regret—and by the items on its "to do" list. The next time you to talk to your friends or work associates about "multitasking," ask them how it makes them feel. Included in their responses will likely be "anxious," "irritable," and "tense." These are often the outcomes resulting from trying to do several things at the same time; such behavior often results in stress and unproductive activity. As the modern world continues to create an increasing number of demands, it creates in turn more and more pressures and conflicts, impacting personal lives, the way we relate to each other, and the way we work. Multitasking is not going away soon: increased awareness enhances our capacity to develop positive ways to respond.

TAKING CARE OF TIME

*To remain as quiet as our original nature—
this is our practice.*

—*Shunryu Suzuki*

Did you ever spill something because your mind was not focused on the present, because you weren't paying attention? Do you know anybody who hasn't? A vivid memory of creating a mess through lack of awareness returns to me again and again over the years, like a continuous wake-up call.

One morning while preparing the breakfast coffee—spooning grounds from the container into the filter—I bumped a spoonful of coffee on the lip of the container. Grounds flew everywhere. "Pay attention," I told myself. And yet, despite this self-admonition, I did it again with the very next spoonful. Frustrated, I put the spoon down, the first step in getting my attention focused. Becoming aware of my mind trying to do several things at once, I took a deep breath and said to myself, "Take care of doing just this one thing."

All the "spills" we create—not just with our hands but in the ocean of personal relationships as well— begin in our own mind. Distracted by the many things we have to do in a brief time, our attention wanders away from taking care of the activity in front of it, becoming concerned instead for finishing the task as quickly as it can so it can move on to another item on its list of priorities. Giving in to distraction, we give up caring about the activity we are doing. And in a subtle but real way, when we do that we also give up caring about our self, about the value of the effort we are making with our life.

Perhaps like never before, a major concern these busy and stressful days is for the lack of time—time to do everything that needs to be done, to do them "on time," and to do them in a quality way. But the real problem for us is not about the scarcity of time— which we can, after all, learn to manage through a variety of strategies. Instead, the real source of suffering is the feeling that "I must get on to something else; this activity is taking too much time." When we have this attitude, we really don't know what we are doing—our mind is somewhere else, not focused on what it earlier decided it needs to take care of. If we don't know what we are doing, how can we be our self? If our mind is *somewhere else*, it means we are trying to *be someone else*, not who we are in the present moment. However, by practicing awareness, we can train ourselves to respond to distractions in a positive way and increase our capacity to give full attention to the task or relationship before us.

The quiet, empty space of zazen reveals the mind's addiction to imagining the future and reminiscing the past. It helps us understand how dwelling in a time other than the present starts to churn the ego: anxieties arise, desires become distractions, and to do things well is nearly impossible. But when there is no idea of time, there are no expectations, and desires do not become a problem.

Meditation teaches us to be careful of allowing ideas of time to interfere with our activity. Through experience, we discover how not to lose our self, but instead to be fully engaged in the "doing" of whatever it is we decided that we must do. Awareness practice is like any other skill-building activity. It is not meant to be casual, or occasional, or reserved for only when convenient. The serious meditation practitioner knows how necessary it is to "sit" every day. That may sound difficult or unappealing, but consider the following possibility:

The forerunner of the modern toothbrush came into use in Egypt sometime around 5,000 years ago. Imagine its introduction to a skeptical society; maybe it went something like this: "Here is the way to reduce tooth decay, gum disease, and mouth odor. But you have to use it every day." Now imagine the response: "Every day! Are you kidding? That's too much. Who has time for that kind of thing!"

These days, only small children complain about brushing. Today we appreciate the benefit of taking time to brush, and to brush well. We understand the serious problems that develop in the long run when we claim to be too "short of time" to brush right now.

By setting aside ideas of how productive or efficient we are in our use of time, we can take time to take care of ourselves physically, emotionally, and spiritually. Meditation is the best way to "manage" time, the best way to prevent spills. Spilling something and making a mess can be a signal that we are too concerned about time and all the things we have to do. Developing the skill to recognize when we are distracted and to return the mind to awareness of the present moment enables us to appreciate our self in all activities.

NEGATIVE TO POSITIVE

A student came to Zen Master Bankei and complained: "Master, I have an ungovernable temper. How can I cure it?"

"You have something very strange," replied Bankei. "Let me see what you have."

"Just now I cannot show it to you," replied the other.

"When can you show it to me?" asked Bankei.

"It arises unexpectedly," replied the student.

"Then," concluded Bankei, "it must not be your true nature. If it were, you could show it to me at any time. When you were born you did not have it, and your parents did not give it to you. Think that over."

—Traditional Zen story

L ike clouds, the individual feelings and emotions that appear in our lives are not predestined to remain with us indefinitely. They come and go, arising and falling in their impermanency. Yet their subsequent half-life—what we might call the length of time they remain in memory—is entirely dependent on our response to them, determining how troublesome they will be to us in the coming years.

Instinctively, we want to turn away from a negative emotion—one that brings psychological discomfort— to deny to ourselves and others that we have the feeling. Or we pretend to "make it go away" by forcing our self to think of something else. However, if we remain in denial of the feeling we experience at the moment, creativity is hampered and life itself is rejected. The most positive response to a painful feeling is straightforward recognition and acknowledgment. Without honest acceptance, the feeling cannot dissipate—we cannot let it go. Then even though it is simply something happening in the moment, we are at risk for endowing it with an artificial sense of permanency, turning it into a heavy stone, an unnecessary burden.

Awareness of the arising or existence of a painful and troubling emotion provides the opportunity to avoid lengthening its life unnecessarily, and so avoid becoming trapped by it. The best first step is to let the mind be contemplative, to simply sit quietly for a few minutes, keeping the mind on the breath. When the "heat" of the emotion has cooled down, admitting—acknowledging in an objective way—that we really do have a particular feeling prepares us to figure out how to resolve the situation that *seems to have created* the emotion in us. Emphasizing *seems to have created*, rather than *did create*, is a vital element of our attitude toward a positive solution. It reflects the understanding that the feeling we have is not the fault of the situation, event, problem, or person confronting us, although it would appear so. Rather, our emotion is a product of our own mind.

Recognition and acceptance of what is going on in our mind is not automatic. We are not always aware, in a conscious sense, of how we feel, especially when under pressure to meet a deadline or any of the other demands of our complex lives. Yet a positive response to a disturbing emotion can only begin with an awareness that surfaces through the sea of distractions. The greater our awareness, the more prepared we are to respond creatively to emotions that continually appear.

WALKING STONES

For we must look about under every stone,
lest an orator bite us.

—Aristophanes

The tenth-century Chinese Zen master Hogen spent a number of years living alone in an old, abandoned temple. One day, four monks on a pilgrimage came to his hermitage and asked if they could stay overnight in the temple courtyard. Hogen agreed, and while the four were building a fire, they discussed philosophical matters, including subjectivity and objectivity. Joining their discussion, Hogen said to them, "Imagine a very large stone. Does it exist inside or outside of your mind?" One of the monks answered, "According to Buddhist teaching, everything is a projection of the mind. So the stone is in my mind." Hogen responded wryly, "Your head must be very heavy carrying around a stone like that in your mind."

Hogen was not denying Buddhist philosophy, nor was he affirming it. He was simply pointing out how heavy is the burden of trying to understand life according to a philosophy—any philosophy—rather than seeing things as they really are, just being present with them without adding our own spin. He was also pointing out the irony that even while the bodies of the traveling monks were moving from place to place, their minds were stuck: heavy, dense, and stubborn like a stone. This story illustrates how people fool themselves by trying to gain understanding through intellectual gymnastics. The mind, being elsewhere rather than in the present moment, becomes immovable and dense as a mountain.

I recall a community project to create a garden in place of the gravel parking lot that existed in front of our own Zen temple. It was a major project. About six months after removing tons of gravel and moving in yards of topsoil, we discovered one morning that someone had left a huge pile of stones in the center of the garden area. We understood that the smooth, beautiful creek stones—varying in shape, size, and color—were left for us with good intentions. We had been offered a gift. But it didn't feel like a gift; it felt like a major burden—just more stones!—an immovable mountain.

I saw this pile of stones as a problem, something in the way of creating our garden, a roadblock to fulfilling our beautiful vision. I wanted the stones gone. At first, I figured we had four options: ask the fellow to take back his stones, haul them ourselves to a vacant lot, try to sell them to a local rockery, or put out a "for free" sign, inviting neighbors to help themselves. After a few weeks, I finally understood how to take care of our so-called "problem": build a stone wall as part of the garden. It took two years to build the wall (there were a great many stones!). Sometimes the neighborhood kids helped out. The wall eventually created a welcoming feeling, leading visitors from the street to the garden path. Through the process of accepting them as an unexpected gift, and turning them from a burden into something useful, I discovered the fluid, moving nature of stones.

Mountains and stones are always appearing in our lives. Changes occur and unwanted things show up; we cannot prevent their happening. If we try to avoid changes, try to push them away, they become heavy and our mind becomes immobile. We have to understand the moving nature of all things. This is the best way to resolve the question of heavy stones.

The great Zen master Dogen, admired for his spiritual insight and poetic sensibilities, declared: "The green mountains are always moving and a stone woman gives birth at night."

How do stones give birth, become alive rather than dense and unmoving? Only when the mind is present, open to various possibilities. Only when it is free from preconceived ideas, ready to respond creatively to whatever appears before it. Otherwise, changes, problems, and unexpected events become heavy and burdensome.

Mountains walk when the mind walks; stones give birth when the mind gives birth. We have to be careful not to let our mind become burdened with the idea of "stones." As Hogen pointed out to his youthful visitors, we have to unburden our mind of stones each moment. This is the nature of spiritual practice.

GETTING OFF THE BUS

*The mass of men lead lives of quiet
desperation. A stereotyped but unconscious
despair is concealed even under what are
called the games and amusements of mankind.*
—Henry David Thoreau

Most people go about their daily lives with a
fair amount of assurance that they have a
good understanding of their world, that
they know how things work and how things and individuals are supposed to behave. Usually, they (and we
too!) do not hesitate to express themselves on any
subject. At the same time, these same people are
secretly not so confident that their experience in
everyday affairs or that their common sense can provide answers to vexing questions that intrude on their
peace of mind: What is the meaning of my life? Does
it have a purpose? Why do we suffer? Is there a God?

The "quiet desperation" Thoreau wrote about is the result of not being able to come to terms with such spiritual concerns.

Buddhism warns us that we cannot understand the larger truths of life by depending solely on the capacity of our analytical mind. Ideas and words cannot help us, nor can formulas or equations. If we try to comprehend Truth with reason and logic, Truth remains obscure. Rational thinking does not allow us to have understanding of Truth in the usual sense because Truth is not a "thing" that can be grasped conceptually. We need to have direct experience of Truth, not isolate our self from it.

It is like trying to know the world from behind the window of a tour bus. How can we appreciate New York, Paris, Yellowstone Park, the mountain, or the desert if we stay on the bus? We have to put our feet on the ground and walk in the place where we find our self. This requires leaving the safety of the bus. It is impossible to know the Truth from a place of security. To really know it for ourselves, we must cultivate the discipline to be willing to let go of the comfort of cherished ideas—of strongly held convictions that prevent us from seeing the world as it is—so that we can have a mind undistorted by desires and prejudices. To come to terms with their quiet desperation, individuals are increasingly turning to the self-disciplined spiritual practice of *selfless* meditation, which is to say meditation devoid of striving for personal gain, which can reveal everything we need to know.

Truth is not something separate and outside our individual being. If we are convinced that it is, we will imagine it to be something that can be acquired, mistakenly turning Truth into a commodity, an object of pursuit. Inevitably what follows is an attempt to create an artificial way to "get it" without the necessary self-exploration and the letting go found through spiritual practice. The result is confusion with techniques that promise a shortcut or quick fix to understanding. We cannot *create* the wisdom—the enlightenment—that is always present, but we can manifest it in our lives with concerted effort. It is like lighting a candle in a dark room: things appear that we did not see before, even though they were there without our awareness.

We are never without complete understanding of the Truth because we are inherently endowed with it. But we become confused on this point when we are not willing to do the work to express it in our attitude and actions, that is, when we want Truth spelled out for us in brief, specific, and uncompromising terms. Seeing the world with this kind of bumper-sticker mentality, we may feel temporary comfort, but soon return to feeling separated from the Truth and from who we are.

The human mind is fascinated with itself. It loves its powers of logic, of connecting ideas, of solving problems, of remembering. In its pride, it deludes itself, seeing the world through the rose-colored glasses of its own ego. Spiritual practice is how we take off the glasses in order to see, without a filter, what we already have. The logical mind should be like a pair of reading glasses: we use them when necessary to get information from a book, then we take them off to see the rest of the world.

If we are to recognize the truth of our life, it won't do to have the world whiz by in a blur. We need to become "lost," to get off the bus and walk around, quietly exploring the side streets and unfamiliar places. To understand our life, we need to pay attention to and appreciate the spaces between the statues, museums, and shrines that we have created. It means acknowledging and accepting our own quiet desperations, becoming intimate with our painful questions. Life is not a sightseeing trip organized for our entertainment. We have to walk around in it so that we can feel its varying textures, the rough as well as the smooth. It is the only way to discover for ourselves the truth of what we are doing with our lives.

BREAKING THE HABIT

*I am deep in my willed habits. From the
outside, I suppose I look like an unoccupied
house with one unconvincing night light left on.*
— *Wallace Stegner*

Do you automatically put an arm under your
pillow when you go to bed at night? When
getting into a pair of pants, is it always right
leg first? When deep in thought, do you fold your
arms across your chest, or look up at the ceiling, or
tap a pencil on the desk? These habits, like most, are
harmless, having no noticeable impact on our lives.
But some habits short-circuit the mind, preventing us
from responding creatively and responsibly to a situation or a relationship that calls for complete presence. Here is where meditation practice can be most
valuable, enabling us to become aware of ingrained,
repetitive, nonproductive reactions to life. Examples

include saying "no" to new ideas out of fear of disrupting a cozy status quo, repeatedly attempting an inappropriate action to resolve a problem, ignoring the evidence of its past failures, or failing to listen to others by not giving them our full attention because of our own restless mind.

Formed by experience, habits are the mind's dependency on actions believed to be successful strategies for "winning" or "defending." Deep-seated memory unconsciously recalls how these strategies have worked before in confusing, uncomfortable, or threatening situations. Having served us well—at least once—in the past, we attach to them, storing them like weapons in our mental armory until they are needed again.

The habit's goal is to make us feel comfortable, to bypass the work required to think through or engage in what should be done or said in the present set of circumstances. A habit—like day-dreaming, a comfortable mental escape—is the opposite of mindfulness, which often includes discomfort when confronting a painful reality embedded in the present situation. By avoiding mental discomfort, habits become a roadblock to creativity.

Rarely is a present situation truly the same as a historical experience. Even if today's problem is the same as yesterday's or last year's, a habitual reaction is at risk for not acknowledging what is going on right now. When that happens, what we say or do can prevent us from creating an appropriate solution or can be harmful to the relationship at hand, thus adding to the problem.

Meditation practice helps break uncreative habit patterns in two ways. By increasing awareness, it helps the mind bring habits into consciousness. By recognizing the habitual reaction as it starts to arise, we have the opportunity to break the short circuit by choosing to bring our attention to the situation and to create an appropriate response, rather than falling back on words or action that might have worked in the past. In addition, because meditation is the practice of "letting go" as well as the practice of awareness, habit patterns may simply fade from the mind without our conscious recognition. Intrinsic in the fading, stubbornness is diminished, replaced by a feeling of mental flexibility and freedom.

FINDING OUR SELF

The mind seems to have the ability to transcend itself and merge with a large presence that feels more real.

—David Brooks

From precivilized to modern times, the record of human history illustrates how humans have consistently maintained a sense of "other" in their lives, a belief or feeling of something intimate with, yet mysteriously beyond, the activities and experiences of daily existence. Religions, rituals, and shamanic practices express the various ways we try to reach out, unite, or be touched by forces greater than our ordinary self. We cannot say for certain to what degree this imaginative energy represents true insight and wisdom about the true nature of Reality, rather than a desire to mitigate suffering and a longing to transcend the limits of finite life—but it is a universal human force, independent of race, geography, or era of time. We should not simply dismiss this yearning as childish or trivial or crazy. The fact is that we continue to reach for what we feel is our essential self, even as it resists precise description. Our worldview—our entire life—is significantly influenced by how we contemplate and relate to the dimensions of our True Self.

In the second of his four noble truths, Buddha carefully explained the singular role of desire and craving in the creation of human suffering. His insight followed his long and strenuous effort to understand both the source and relief of suffering. Soon after Siddhartha Gotama, the historical Buddha, left his palace home around the age of nineteen, he studied with a series of Yoga teachers. Religious historian Karen Armstrong has explained how his first teacher emphasized ignorance—lack of understanding of our True Self, of who we really are—as the source of suffering. In that teacher's philosophy, we suffer because we confuse our True Self with the mental and emotional activities of our ordinary mind. Freedom from suffering takes place through deep awareness of the eternal True Nature, independent and beyond temporary emotional states of ordinary life. True Nature, Gotama was instructed, is potential in everybody but it is hidden by the phenomenon of the everyday world. The practice of the yogi ascetics that he met was aimed at simplifying life by leaving society, avoiding distractions, cultivating the intellect, contemplating the teachings, and practicing the meditative disciplines. Only then does True Nature replace the small self and freedom from suffering is achieved, he was taught.

In his ascetic practices, Gotama experienced elevated states of consciousness, including a state of nothingness. However, when he came out of meditative trance, he still felt desire, fear, and passion. It happened with every subsequent teacher he studied with and with every practice. Aware of the pattern, the perceptive future Buddha realized that what he experienced in meditation was not his True Self and that there was still more to understand. Eventually, he went off on his own and discovered how the True Self is not separate from the ordinary self, that is, from the self that becomes confused, anxious, or impatient. And he understood how spiritual practice is not about trying to annihilate human tendencies but rather to understand them with gentle acceptance. He discovered that True Nature exists in midst of the mundane, not separate from it.

Consider the following parable, attributed to the Indian yogi Paramahansa Yogananda, which illustrates the need for reorienting our view of our self in order to recognize who we really are:

A lioness, in the latter stages of pregnancy, becomes weak from lack of food. She stalks a flock of sheep and as she gets close, she leaps at one. Just at that moment she gives birth to a cub and dies from weakness and the ordeal. The orphaned cub has no choice but to join the flock of sheep, learning to eat grass and bleat.

Months later, another hungry lion comes stalking the flock. It is astonished to see an adolescent lion eating grass and bleating. The frightened flock and the young sheep-lion flee. The hunting lion calls out, "Stop running away; you are a lion." The sheep-lion bleats, "NO! I'm not!" So the hunting lion takes the young lion to a lake and shows him his reflection in the still water. Then he lets out a load roar. The young sheep-lion copies him with a roar of his own. Now he no longer believes he is a sheep; he knows he is a lion.

Sometimes we have this kind of experience. We live our life in delusion, not recognizing that we are not living as who we really are but as who we think we are, as we are conditioned to see our self. We may encounter somebody who enables us to look at our self in new way. Usually this encounter is spontaneous, unplanned: we meet someone without seeking and so have no preconceived expectations. At other times, the meeting is planned, as when we choose a school because of its well-known teachers and we expect to learn something useful, something that will help us, that will add to our understanding. In either case, if we pay attention and do the required work, we will be influenced, we will expand our worldview, and we will better understand ourselves.

To find our True Self requires effort; it is not a simple thing to free our self from our self, from long-held behaviors, desires, and notions of who we think we are. There are no shortcuts. In the parable, the sheep-lion had to do more than have his face shown to him. He had to roar to become himself. This sounds like it was easy; after all, a lion is supposed to roar. But if we carefully examine our own life, we will discover that we may have the same problem the lion-sheep had: he was confused about who he really was. Truly being who we are, living in accordance with our True Self, eludes us. It is why we humans have such yearning for discovering our greater self.

Manifesting our true self requires effort and discipline. It is not easy to end a life-long habit of bleating, to have the courage to roar, to let go of ideas about our self, and to experience our True Self. We can be led by someone to the edge of knowing, to see a reflection of our self. But each of us has to learn to roar.

ENLIGHTENED COMMUNICATION

You give but little when you give of your possessions. It is when you give of yourself that you truly give.

—*Kahlil Gibran*

Most of us are confident in our capacity to communicate well. We hardly ever think about it; we assume that we speak accurately and appropriately and that we listen without distortion. When we are reflective and not biased by emotion, there is no problem. Difficulties arise when our knowledge or understanding is lacking or when we are unaware of feelings that color, filter, or reshape what we say or hear.

Many of us make the common mistake of assuming that we will recognize the impact that our words and actions will have on others. But the recognition is not automatic. Our mind is too easily distracted by the lightning speed of our own thoughts and emotions, and by a never-ending kaleidoscope of events and concerns. Too often we fail to notice a subtle response—a word or a look—that would otherwise tell us we have said or done something that has resulted in a feeling we did not intend. So we are always at risk for saying or doing something that we later regret, that we wish we could take back. The painful feeling of regret is actually fortunate, accompanying the vital recognition that something we did or said is likely to have hurt a relationship. This knowing provides the opportunity to respond creatively, to do something to clarify the misunderstanding. Unfortunately, the recognition often escapes us and the misunderstanding remains.

Increasing our awareness skill increases our chances of minimizing communication problems and interpersonal conflicts in two ways.

In Figure 1, the "Event" represents something we did or said that created a problem or misunderstanding, without our immediate recognition of its negative impact. The "Recognition" occurs at a later time: minutes, days, even months or years.

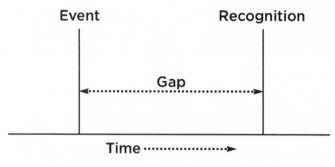

Figure 1

With increased awareness, we recognize more "Events": fewer things we say or do pass by without eventual recognition. In addition, the time lag, the "Gap" between the "Event" and the "Recognition," decreases, as shown in Figure 2:

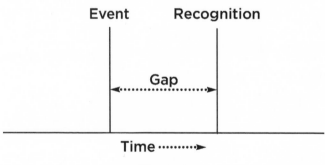

Figure 2

As our awareness capacity continues to increase, the "Gap" continues to decrease, so that "Recognition" occurs closer and closer to the "Event." When the "Gap" diminishes completely, "Recognition" occurs as the "Event" is beginning to take place, so that we catch ourselves *as we start* to say or do something. The "Event" remains unborn in the mind, not expressed in word or deed. The result is fewer misunderstandings and fewer conflicts, less harm created in the world. The process is of course not quite as mechanical as the diagrams might suggest. Increased awareness is accompanied by increased sensitivity to situations and people. We develop a subjective sense, a wider view, of how our words and actions might affect others.

When we think of saintly people, we imagine them to be omniscient in thought, without distraction, never troubled by emotions. Yet the person we consider saintly is, like the rest of us, most likely not free of emotional "buttons." Rather, he or she has developed his or her awareness so that "Recognition" occurs instantaneously and the mind remains calm. The waves do not appear on the surface; there is no "Event."

With practice, this capacity is available to all of us.

A SENSE OF CONTROL

The impotence of man to govern or restrain
  the emotions I call bondage,
for a man who is under their control is not his
  own master.

—*Baruch Spinoza*

All living things instinctively strive to control the areas of their lives they consider essential to survival and peace of mind. As individuals and societies, we safeguard our home, protect food and water supplies, and establish rules of behavior for the benefit of our children and our community. Making an effort to control certain elements of life is natural and necessary. But when we are anxious or when we are greedy, the desire to have control over all relationships—whether with people, things, or nature itself—can be exceedingly strong. It can dominate a life.

I ask the students in the "Meditation at Work" class I teach, "On a scale of zero to 100, how much of life do you feel you can control?" The average of the group response is usually in the 30 to 40 percent range. The majority recognize that we have little control of most elements of life. Except in rare situations where we have in our possession a resource that gives us clearly recognized power to control the behavior, thinking, or well-being of others, we are not the lone decision-maker. Few of us attain sufficient wealth, strength, or knowledge to make unilateral decisions from a position of nearly complete control. For the majority, almost all situations involve negotiation, some kind of give and take. We may not have control, but what we do have in each situation—based on what we do or say—is influence.

Parents and schoolteachers know how difficult it is to control the behavior of young children by just trying to be "the boss" and many have discovered more creative ways influence their behavior—to everyone's benefit. Of course, this does not mean that we should treat each other as children, but rather as equals, with respect and attention. Relationships are always changing, sometimes suddenly, at other times in small, subtle ways that escape our notice. To keep a relationship stable and productive when it is changing, we may have to modify what we do or say. But first we have to actually notice that something *has* changed. Constantly scheming to find ways to control events and people in the world around us produces stress, stubbornness, and a narrow vision of life. A more creative strategy is available: we can pay attention to what is going on and to our own attitude, to how we can adapt ourselves to a changing situation so that we can maintain a relationship or achieve a desired result, without feeling we need to be the "boss." Then we are in control in a large sense in a world that is constantly changing. We all have this power; each of us is ultimately the lone decision-maker of our actions and our words.

Increasing awareness capacity helps reorient our emphasis from control, which is rare, to influence, which is always available. The greater our skill of awareness, the greater our chances of recognizing a subtle feeling of being out of control or noticing when something has changed or is changing. The sharp focus of recognition gives us the opportunity to determine a productive response. We can ask our self, "What can I do or say to influence this situation?"

At the end of a difficult day when, despite our best efforts, a problem was not resolved or a new problem arose, rather than carrying around the heavy baggage of feeling out of control, we can go home with some confidence knowing that we have the capacity to respond in a creative way to stressful situations—even though we may not always be as successful as we would like.

We know that tomorrow we can again try, with patience and openness born of our spiritual practice, to influence issues whose solutions are not yet clear.

CONTINUOUS EFFORT

Divinity must live within herself:
Passions of rain, or moods in falling snow;
Grievings in loneliness or unsubdued
Elations when the forest blooms.

—*Wallace Stevens*

A number of years ago, the film critic Roger Ebert commented on the public excitement created by the release of *Star Wars: The Phantom Menace*. Before the film arrived in the theaters, people were camping in long lines for expensive tickets and choice seats. This extraordinary enthusiasm was the result of the movie touching people in a spiritual way, Ebert explained. It has myths, heroism, overcoming evil, and wisdom. "It even contains some Zen Buddhism!" he said.

When a film—or a book or a play—excites our spirituality, we wake up to a part of our self that gets overlooked in the rush of everyday affairs. But after the movie, then what? After the occasional weekend retreat, what next? Spiritual encouragement coming from outside our self cannot last for long. Like candy or the biblical apple, the taste—the sweet "rush"— soon fades. To feel the depth of spirituality, we need to feel encouraged from inside.

Months or years afterward, we may remember the good feeling we had at the movie. Nevertheless, unless we maintain spiritual practice, inspiration is just a one-time treat. But spirituality is more than special treats or exciting experiences. When practice is continuous, we do not require candy bars or special events to inspire us. Then everything we do has the background of spiritual practice; everything feels special, not just one thing or one experience. Although we may act foolishly at times, if we continue our spiritual practice, it will keep our mind settled, allowing us to see beyond foolishness. We will recognize the inherent wisdom and perfection in everyone. This was Buddha's experience.

Much of the growing interest in meditation comes from the somewhat mistaken notion that meditation is a process of purifying oneself, a way of transforming the "impure," troublesome aspects of our personality. "If I can transform myself and get rid of my impurities," goes the logic, "I won't have any more troubles, I won't have to make any more effort to constantly fight them, and I will be happy."

Humans have always dreamed of transforming themselves, of becoming "pure," of gaining freedom from the "impurities" of the human condition. For many, this yearning can be a desire of great force, a hopeful vision of a "pure" state of being, existing apart from everyday life. It rests on the anxious feeling that one is basically "impure," as well as belief in a spiritual alchemy with the power to "purify" us into something other than who we are in this moment. The misunderstanding is based on the mind's stubborn tendency to fool itself. Rather than trying to transform our self from "impure" to "pure" we would be wiser to make a continuous effort to express our inherent positive qualities in the midst of the changing, confusing, often unfair situations that life presents to us.

A well-known Zen story tells of the Zen teacher Nangaku asking his disciple Baso why he is sitting in zazen. Baso answers that he is trying to become a Buddha—and so Nangaku then picks up a brick and starts to rub it with a second brick. Baso asks his teacher why he is doing that, to which Nangaku replies that he is making a mirror. When Baso then asks how Nangaku can make a brick into a mirror, Nangaku asks, "And how can you become a Buddha by doing zazen?" His meaning and his message to us is: "You cannot transform yourself into something else. Be who you already are."

No matter how much we grind it, a brick can never be perfectly smooth. Just like that brick, no matter how much we polish our self, there will always remain some surface roughness. However, as the ancient story tries to demonstrate, we are already inherently "pure," even with our roughness. Yet this doesn't mean that we need not pay attention to our life and not try to smooth our rough spots when we recognize how they create problems for our self and others. Nangaku did not tell Baso to stop polishing himself, only to understand the real meaning of his determined effort.

OUT OF SIGHT, OUT OF MIND

I took a trip on a train and I thought about you.
—*Frank Sinatra*

You can see it from the train in New York and New Jersey, outside Philadelphia and Chicago, throughout Europe, and from Tokyo to Kyoto: old cars, oil drums, broken furniture, decomposing lumber, rusting metal parts, obsolete appliances all meant to be placed out of sight where they can be easily ignored, perhaps with the hope that somehow they will go away.

The collections of discards and decaying ruins are like our disappointments, old painful stuff that nobody really wants to look at. We seem incapable of disposing of them or of returning them to their natural state. The fronts of the houses and buildings we see from the train are well kept, showing their best faces to the world—much like we ourselves do. But the messy, disturbing material is hidden away out back. Ignoring the painful is tempting, a comfortable approach to life, even as we know we need to take care not to clutter our landscapes—internal and external—with trash.

We often comfort ourselves by saying, "Life is not always fair"—as if we were contending with a devious, unscrupulous opponent. We use this as an aphorism for the unexpected events that shatter plans and dreams. All lead to disappointment, a pain we would prefer to escape, rather than confront. Yet taking the comfortable approach—forcing a failed expectation out of mind—only leads to discouragement and greater suffering in the long run. Our spiritual well-being requires that we not put disappointments out back. When they occur, we need to accept them as part of our life experience, to learn from them, and to develop the confidence that they will not get in our way.

Confidence arises from knowing that disappointments do not change who we are, rather that our fundamental nature remains the same no matter what happens day to day. With this wisdom, we are always ready for the next effort.

Disappointments emerge not only from the objective world—from nature's fickleness and from the surprises, even betrayals, of other people. We ourselves are also the source of our disappointments—through our own inevitable mistakes and misjudgments—

when we do not meet a personal goal. Yet there exists even a third, rarely acknowledged, type of disappointment. These are not the kind that happen to us; they occur when we disappoint the world. The foundation of our spirituality is based on not disappointing our collective world.

At times we promise to do something helpful for others, by volunteering assistance, or agreeing to give it when asked. With a sense of responsibility we then do the best we can to meet the expectation of others and not disappoint them. But the most vital quality of spirituality occurs *before* we make a personal promise or recite a vow. It is the attitude based on the understanding that the entire world is dependent on us not to disappoint, but instead to express our inherent unselfish nature, the self that does not collect disappointments.

Suffering results from allowing our life to be run by the expectations we put on the objective, external world. Spirituality has a different orientation: it emphasizes the expectation we place on our self to live according to our true nature and so to not disappoint our world. Through spiritual practice we learn how to prevent a personal disappointment from becoming trash on the landscape.

THE MEANING OF COURTESY

*And there was knowing that twice since
midnight a person had trusted me enough to
fall asleep beside me.*

—John Updike

The first Zen Buddhist wedding that I attended closed with the words: "Courtesy decorates the world; every phenomenon, an instructor." What a cold-water shock I felt hearing this: I lost mental balance; my mind spun, unable to grasp a thing, as if I had suddenly awakened in a strange, unfamiliar world. The experience was my first recognition of how *courtesy*—true courtesy—was not simply what my mother taught me about being polite, not merely the advice of Emily Post or Miss Manners. Its real meaning, I discovered, is spiritual; its origin is selflessness.

Even superficial courtesy, if only for a moment, orients us toward others, interrupting concern for our own gratification, a concern that can be an obsessive tendency, a very strong emotional pull, its beginnings often beyond our control. Although it may not have been our fault at its start, we need determination to go beyond the obsession—the overriding anxiety for our own comforts and pleasures—and the limitations it puts on our response to life, our sense of well-being, and our relationships with others.

However, true courtesy requires us to remain mindful in our daily actions and to come back to the present when we notice attention has strayed. Without this willingness to come back from distraction, courtesy is lost. Zen Master Dogen recognized the importance of courtesy as an expression of selflessness, complaining of mindless monks who were "careless of greetings and bows."

Former president Harry Truman had a sense of the fundamental courtesy that is more than simple politeness. His biography describes his daily walks, part of the routine he established following his retirement to his home in Independence, Missouri. Passing an enormous gingko tree on Maple Street, his biographer tells us, Truman would customarily speak to it. *"You're doing a good job,"* he'd say.

Truman's was not an act of superficial courtesy. Rather, it was an expression of the inherent, universal courtesy that exists everywhere, reflecting the understanding that everything is doing its best in accordance with everything else. Even though Truman was criticized for being unsophisticated and at times a bit crude, he knew how to "greet and bow." Years after he died, he was recognized as having been perhaps one of our best presidents.

Thoughtful, selfless courtesy is more than a brief gesture, polite word, or forced smile. The eleventh-century Chinese Zen master Fuyo Dokai advised, "Stop longing for fame and gain; regard everything you see as a flower growing on a rock." This reverence for all things is a reflection of inherent courtesy. It is the ultimate expression of spiritual practice. It is compassion itself, extending beyond the transient meeting of the moment.

Courtesy in its true, fundamental sense is not about making people like us. It is not meant to manipulate or seduce others to gain their approval. On the contrary, it is beyond gaining something for our self.

Through spiritual practice, we can come to truly appreciate the meaning of selfless, fundamental courtesy.

COMING DOWN FROM THE ATTIC

This day will not come again.
Each minute is worth a priceless gem.

—*Zen Master Takuan*

had lost track of him and we had not spoken to one another in more than a dozen years—so I was surprised by the handwritten letter from my old friend. The lightness and humor of his words showed he discovered how to put past difficulties behind him. He had a new job, a new family, and a different way of seeing himself. One memorable line in his note precisely and poignantly encapsulated the human condition: "I know now that life is rich and full of opportunities to learn, if only I can just get out of the way." Reading his revelation, I wondered if anyone experiencing this understanding for the first time could avoid feeling remorse over lost opportunities and lack of direction.

How do we "get in the way" of our own life? What do we mean—what is it that we sense—when we say such things?

Growing up on the crowded, noisy streets of New York, I looked forward to the Sunday train ride from Grand Central Station to suburban Port Chester, the monthly visit to Grandma. She was spending her remaining years with my aunt and uncle in a nondescript, two-story clapboard house whose grandeur, to this ten-year-old, compared favorably with the Chrysler Building. Best of all, it had an attic, sheltering treasures and relics of the past—early-twentieth-century appliances, furniture, tools, books, photographs, clothes—that once had a life but were now at rest. I found a curious tranquillity rummaging in the dusty world of dim old things whose original meaning I could only imagine. Attics have that kind of magic. On almost every visit, my mother came to the foot of the attic stairs to remind me why we were in Port Chester: "Come down now and spend some time with Grandma."

I have learned that we have to come down from the attic, that we have to let old things be old and pay attention to things of the present. By remaining in the cramped and crowded relics of the past, the mind creates its own stagnation, limiting life by continuing ancient habit patterns. Sifting and sorting, always reviewing antique material, foraging in the stuff of times long gone, we may feel nostalgic and comforted.

But it is a dusty, boxed-in place where nothing is new. Staying stuck in the dust, our sense of our life becomes, "I *am* my past."

My friend's letter graphically illustrated the suffering inherent in the painful recognition of feeling "stuck" in life. But after the recognition appears, then what? What do we do when we become aware of our own suffering?

Almost mysteriously, a second letter, closely following and much like the first, from another friend from whom I also had not heard in years, provided part of the answer. He wrote, "I have to be vigilant that I do not fall into my habitual karmic pattern." This is an important insight: letting go of old habits does not come automatically, without the work of paying attention.

The vigilance my second friend wrote about is not the usual armed, on-guard watchfulness associated with early-warning detection of the enemy "out there." Instead, it is referring to a softer, inward awareness of the tendencies of our own mind, the one cultivated in meditative practice that enables us to leave the attic by bringing mindfulness to the present moment.

In their own ways, my two friends discovered that meditation is like opening the windows of a dusty attic to let freshness flow in. When the mind is not refreshed it becomes stubborn and biased, making us feel that we are "in the way." It is like water that does not move—becoming stagnant and poisonous—where nothing lives and nothing grows. The refreshed mind—like flowing water—continually supports life.

And all this can spring from the simple practice of maintaining awareness of the continual coming and going of our flowing breath. That specific, simple, quietly observant activity opens the door to the more boundless awareness of flowing life. When the mind is always present in that universal flow—when we are down from the attic—we can never feel "in the way" of our self.

TUNING OUR LIFE

Come learn with me the fatal song
Which knits the world in music strong;
Come lift thine eyes to lofty rhymes,
Of things with things, of times with time.
—*Ralph Waldo Emerson*

leet and brown slush covered the streets, as snow fell heavily from a gray sky in twenty-degree weather. A typical New York winter day, far too nasty for playing in the streets. Several of our adolescent crowd took refuge in the warmth of our friend's family brownstone on the West Side. We played games, listened to records, and just horsed around, as energetic preteenage boys do whenever the opportunity arises. When the streetlights came on, our friend's mother interrupted our play: "Time for your violin, Freddie. Boys, you'll have to go home now."

The others went home, but out of curiosity, I asked if I could stay to watch Freddie practice. I watched in silence as he carefully tuned up his instrument, plucking each string in turn, tightening and loosening its peg to obtain the proper note. Back and forth he went between strings, plucking, listening, and adjusting with singular attention. Freddie's effort to fine-tune his instrument, I felt, must be one of life's most boring activities. I didn't understand why he put up with it. Yet, he seemed to like doing it; he remained intent and focused. He told me he tuned up his violin every day.

I was glad I didn't play the violin, to have to do all that tuning up. It was too much work; it interfered with playing in the streets, with having a good time, not something that a normal, lively young boy would want to do. Stringed instruments don't work well if they are not tuned with care. Too loose, the string makes a dull, deathly sound. Too tight, it yields a squeaky, skin-crawling vibration. And all the strings must be tuned in harmony, otherwise they create noise rather than music. Yet I was struck by the realization that my friend didn't seem to mind and wondered how that possibly could be so.

I have since learned that life works much the same way as stringed instruments. Each human being is like a violin, capable of beautiful music. But just like Freddie's violin, it is very easy to fall out of tune. And it is never certain that we will be "in tune" to a new situation, to some change in our life—to what minor

changes might have occurred that gradually transformed in tune into out of tune. So each of us needs to
pay attention to the sounds we make with our life, to
make the effort to be "in tune" if we want our lives to
go well. We know we are in tune when we feel no separation from ourselves, from each other, from what
we are doing, from life all around us. When we are in
tune, we feel we are the harmonious music of a finely
tuned orchestra.

Life has many dimensions—as do we ourselves.
Composed of many strings, we express ourselves in a
variety of ways. If we want to make music with our
life, rather than noise, we need to be tuned in all ways,
not just in some, and in all moments, not merely some
of the time.

What prevents us from being in tune? What dis-
tracts us from paying attention, from tuning our self
to our life? In part, it is the gullible, unreflective
notion that we are already in tune. We create problems for ourselves when we believe we are somehow,
automatically, sufficiently in tune, when we are
unwilling to make the effort to be aware, to pay attention to how we are doing right now. Like the young
boy not understanding the need to make that effort,
the notion "I am not interested in tuning up" means
we have determined to settle for a noisy life of dishar-
mony. But when we are not willing to settle for a life
of discord, we turn to spiritual practice to understand

how we can make the music that we are inherently capable of creating.

Zazen is the process of continually tuning our self. It is how we find harmony with our life and with others. When we ourselves are in tune, the entire world feels in tune. As my friend's violin practice demonstrated, spiritual practice includes doing the tuning up our self. There can be no appeal to someone else to do the work of tuning up our own life.

Every one of our daily activities is an opportunity to create music with our life. It appears in our continuous tuning practice, through listening to ourselves and feeling the sound of the relationships between ourselves and others. But we are easily distracted and fail to recognize the noise, so we have to continually encourage our self to tune our self.

Over sixty years ago, I witnessed a caring mother encourage her son to learn to create music, to set aside playing for a while, to pay attention to tuning up. It remains a warm memory, a reminder of the power of ordinary events and their capacity to be metaphors for the larger life.

ASKING THE RIGHT QUESTION

*All this struggling and striving to make the
world better is a great mistake; not because it
isn't a good thing to improve the world if you
know how to do it, but because striving and
struggling is the worst way you could set
about doing anything.*

—*George Bernard Shaw*

Three years ago, I attended a symposium sponsored by a local interfaith organization. The question for consideration that evening was, "How does your religion or faith repair the world?" The question demonstrated the good intention of the symposium and the sincerity of the organizers. Yet, when I first read it, I felt something missing. On reflection, I realized that the wording lacked a sense of intimacy.

When it came my turn to say something, I reframed the question in a way that held more meaning for me: "How do we respond to suffering in the world?" I actually think this is the question we all need to explore, individually and collectively. It requires us to recognize that each of us has an active role in the presence of universal suffering that is never beyond our reach. The question asks us to consider how we are to take care of each other on this planet, both near at hand and far away. When we accept this as our universal question we can then inquire how our various religions and spiritual practices can help us find answers.

Our personal attitude toward our role of "taking care" in this world is vital. The capacity to take care is an inherent human quality, yet it is easy to forget or ignore, to lose our way within everyday concerns. This is what the symposium was all about, for it is within religious practice that we remind ourselves of our responsibility to each other and discover how to nurture our care-taking attitude.

There is danger in trying to identify ways to "repair" the world. The effort forces us to see the world in a mechanical way, fundamentally broken—with us holding the wrench. It is a viewpoint that puts us at risk for becoming arrogant, for insisting that "our way" provides the necessary fix according to our assessment of the problem in need of repair. We would be better off considering a friendlier, more spacious, question: "What can we do to enable the world to heal itself?" This viewpoint of the world as a living organism brings us close, minimizing the danger of intrusion. It also provides insight into our own spiritual nature.

Yet sometimes in life things do need to be "fixed"—a broken arm needs to be reset, a person in danger needs to be rescued, victims of a flood, fire, or drought need helping hands. But our work in life is not limited by mechanics, by only repairing things after they break. The work begins before breakage occurs, with the continuous effort to prevent suffering by taking care of relationships with them.

We nurture our inherent healing capacity through selfless spiritual practice, the vehicle for experiencing the world as it is—and ourselves as we are—without interference from the self-oriented tendency of our mind. Selfless practice has no personal goal, no expectations of attaining anything for one's self. It is how we resume our sense of oneness with each other and with all things. When there is unity rather than separation, all things are healed.

But emphasis on spiritual practice as the foundation for healing doesn't mean we just sit there and passively let the world go by. It doesn't mean that we do not intervene when necessary, that there is no social action. It means that our helping activities need to be based on the compassion of a care-taking attitude, rather than on whatever fix we imagine we can apply. For without compassion as the basis, we can easily develop self-pride in our "fix" and create separation from the very ones in need of help.

We can be charitable to others in a number of ways, sometimes through physical activity and volunteer work, sometimes with money. Sometimes we do it face to face, sometimes we do it for people we will never meet. This is the "quantitative" side of selflessness: it can be measured in hours, dollars, and number of clients. However, the foundation of helping is spiritual, unmeasurable. It is treating others as our self, giving our self by giving up our self. We do it through patience and listening, treating everyone with equal respect, not trying to gain control or take advantage, not letting emotions overwhelm us when they start to arise, maintaining creative, healthy relationships, and by keeping our eyes open for ways to lend a hand. We do it as well with our environment by not destroying unnecessarily and not polluting the air we all must breathe and the water we all must drink.

Selflessness is the way we can experience the sanctity of all things, the necessary ground for treating our shared world with respect.

Based on active spiritual practice, it is our way of "healing" the world, including both our response to suffering and the prevention of it.

THE HIGH ROAD

You take the high road
and I'll take the low road
And I'll be in Scotland before you.
                    —Traditional Scottish ballad

T his song suggests more than a young man's heartbreak over the loss of his sweetheart. It reflects a universal lament for the seeming disappearance of a fundamental attribute of life. The apparent absence is replaced by a yearning so deep that life is diminished by an unremitting distress for what has been lost, a constant quest for the road home. We want the feeling of being on the "high road": complete, secure, embraced by the world, and confident of our future. And we want clarity about the meaning of life and our role in it. But it is a characteristic of the modern world that much—perhaps most—of humanity feels disoriented, as if having emerged from the subway into the shadows of a strange neighborhood. We have a sense of being on the low road, without recall of how we arrived. We yearn to return to the high road. Yet the actual truth is that we have never really gone far from that road— it's just that we don't know it. Allowing ourselves to be distracted and misled by our own desires, we misread the world we live in. Not recognizing the spiritual side of ourselves, of True Nature, we feel that something is missing, that we are lost in unfamiliar territory.

The distractions of the modern world are intense, accelerated by skilled advertising. Alluring pictures of attractive commodities make very seductive promises. And we are vulnerable, susceptible to the promises, thinking, "These things will satisfy my empty feeling and I will be on the high road to a good life." Our problem is failure to recognize the source of our confusion: perceptions of reality and life distorted by desire for material and emotional things. We become spiritually ill when we feel entitled to possess whatever the everyday world promises. Feeling entitled to be "high" and on the "high road," we are an easy mark for disappointment and suffering.

Our not knowing is the low road, and this is the basis of our delusion. The true "high road" is not about feeling high; rather, it is resting in satisfaction with the world we are in, with what we already have, unconcerned for what we do not have. Avoiding the artificial while embracing and being embraced by the real, the natural and authentic, in our everyday world—moonlight, rain, forests, bird songs, oranges, decaying leaves, lizards, the ocean—takes us to the high road, as Willa Cather shows us in *My Antonia*:

> The earth was warm under me, and warm as I crumbled it through my fingers…. I kept as still as I could. Nothing happened. I did not expect anything to happen. I was something that lay under the sun and felt it, like the pumpkins, and I did not want to be anything more. I was entirely happy. Perhaps we feel like that when we die and become part of something entire, whether it is sun and air, or goodness and knowledge. At any rate, that is happiness; to be dissolved into something complete and great. When it comes to one, it comes as naturally as sleep.

The good news is that each of us has the capacity for this embrace. The other part of the good news is that there is no bad news—life only asks us to remain mindful so that Reality can appear. This is the role of contemplative spiritual practice: enabling our intellectual machinery to relax its grip on mental images and fixed ideas so that anxieties can lose their intensity.

With continuous practice, so much is revealed about desires, dependencies, and the lure of artificial promises. It discloses the road we think we are on and how we create it. Our encounter with our imagined low road leads us to the high road, providing the chance to explore unexplored and scary places—the mental back alleys and dead ends between the monuments and edifices we conceive with our yearnings. Facing the low road with determination—facing our self—is itself the high road.

Delusions are always with us. Yet, keeping spiritual practice alive in the midst of ever-recurring desires shows us this very fact is the path to wholeness. To see life as a single road is to return home at every step.

COMPOSURE

HAPPINESS

We hold these truths to be self-evident, that all men are created equal, that they are endowed by their creator with certain unalienable rights, that among these are Life, Liberty, and the Pursuit of Happiness.

—The Constitution of the
United States of America

The core of the American revolution was the vision of freedom, the unrestricted capacity to create a life of satisfaction, of happiness. What was once fought over and died for is today taken for granted, an unquestioned precept of democracy. But do we understand the real meaning of "happiness"? Do we know what will satisfy us, what it is we should "pursue"? And do we really understand how to conduct our lives so that we will be happy in the truest sense?

The "right" to pursue happiness is a political "right," a fundamental freedom in a democratic society, protected by law. No one has the right to deprive another of the right to pursue his or her own happiness. At the same time, although we are guaranteed a right to pursue it in our own fashion, happiness is neither a privilege nor an entitlement. Each of us has to discover the meaning of true happiness.

We might say that happiness must be "earned," but that would also not be fully accurate. Such a description turns happiness into a commodity, a reward. To speak of happiness as something to be *realized* is closer to the truth. The point is simple but often unrecognized: our own effort is required. To wait for happiness to be handed to us is a big misunderstanding as well as a source, ironically, of unhappiness. In order to realize happiness, we must first understand the basis for happiness, and for unhappiness as well. Zazen emphasizes continuously returning to awareness of the present, including the state of our own mind. The practice enables us to notice when we are fooling ourselves with preconceived, unexamined ideas of happiness.

The awakened, subtle mind recognizes the oneness inherent in every relationship as well as the need to practice accommodation, to "find our fit," in each of them.

One person cannot make another person happy; we cannot be passive and let someone else do our work. It is a mistake to expect a guru, a teacher, a mentor, or a lover to fix our problem of unhappiness. If we fall into that trap, we will eventually blame that person when our problem doesn't "go away," succumbing to the deluded notion, "My unhappiness is somebody else's fault."

Pursuing objects on our happiness list is unnecessary, and worse, it creates a life of unquenchable desire. People who live life constantly trying to fulfill desires are known in Buddhism as "hungry ghosts"—spirits endlessly seeking food that can never even begin to sate their hunger.

Happiness begins with awareness, increasing the subtleness of the mind that understands the source of unhappiness, the nature of its own compulsions and desires. With that wisdom the mind can move from self-orientation to selflessness, the ultimate home of happiness.

TRUTH IN THE ORDINARY

And nobody gets out of it, having to swim through the fires to stay in this world.

                                                        —*Mary Oliver*

We are attracted to what appear to be mystical qualities that might unlock secrets of the spiritual world, providing us personal enlightenment. However, exciting as they may be, these pursuits can only take us a small part of the way in our efforts to understand Reality and the truth of our own life. Eventually we realize that we must go beyond the intellectual and the mystical, beyond words, and engage in the practice itself.

When we are new to Zen or any spiritual practice, we may believe that it will provide us with something extraordinary, something absent in our lives. Yet after we have practiced, with regularity, for a time, we perceive that there is nothing external to be obtained, that we already have what we seek only do not recognize it. And we also realize that it is not unique to our individual self: it is universal, shared by everyone and everything. This understanding is accompanied by a sense of well-being and freedom. Little by little, we let go of trying to attain something special, learning instead to experience satisfaction and fulfillment in the ordinary activities of our daily lives: eating, sweeping, cooking, cleaning the toilet, being with other people, listening to or giving a presentation at work, answering the telephone. This is the secret of spiritual practice and of life: within the world's ordinariness resides the expression of Truth. By not recognizing or accepting this simple point, we make our lives quite complicated.

We create problems for ourselves when we view our life through an artificial prism of self-orientation. When that happens, we worry we will not get what we want, putting our minds in turmoil by striving to gain recognition, becoming anxious when problems arise, asking, "Why do I have to suffer?" We think and feel this way when we are convinced of our own importance, when we see our self as a princess or a king. And like royalty, we act as if the world is conspired against us when our desires are unmet. However, when we let go of the notion of our own importance, we feel fulfilled in our ordinary activities. There is no longer an important self to defend or fight for and we are free to engage playfully in our everyday world. This kind of understanding is not intellectual; it is the wisdom of a fluid mind that observes the way things are.

When this happens, the problem of self-importance and personal ambition is transformed into the peace and confidence that comes with humility. We understand and we accept that no one of us is more special than anyone else. Each of us has his or her own skills, talents, history, imperfections, and concerns. In our discriminating mind, these characteristics usually make us feel separate from one another. Yet being ordinary, shared, human qualities, they actually unite us when we do not make judgments.

When we approach each moment of our life without an agenda, we do not feel pressure to prove our specialness through a continual, lifelong process of acquisition. We start each day as a novice, with anticipation, recognizing that no one is an expert at being alive. On the other hand, holding on to a feeling of importance or expertise creates an expectation that the world will acknowledge, respect, and praise us. When the world does not respond as we would like, we become angry at it for holding back what we feel we deserve and so create our own suffering. This suffering is in direct proportion to the self-importance we feel.

As we practice and learn to do things with a mind of nonattachment, that is, without desire for material or emotional payoff, our "doing"—performing physical labor, creating art, solving a problem, relating

with people—will naturally express the highest quality that we are capable of providing. And we will find
satisfaction in everything we do. So rather than create
problems of "specialness," we are wise to find our
true self in ordinariness and selflessness.

Our inherent enlightenment is expressed when
there are no strings attached to what we do.

A MEANINGFUL LIFE

After all, after all we have endured, who has grown wise?

—Robinson Jeffers

We have to ask ourselves, "What kind of life is meaningful? How do I balance pursuit of personal goals with the expression of my life as something greater than myself? What do I do to avoid becoming overwhelmed by desire for the benefits of material progress?"

The incentive to be successful is one of the most powerful qualities of humanity, energizing our creativity and inspiring us to engage our activity for the benefit of others. Yet there is a paradox within the motivation to succeed, for if we are not careful, we can be seduced by the almost universal misunderstanding that personal success automatically provides happiness and peace of mind. By paying careful attention to our own experience, we have a chance to realize that just the opposite is true, that the desire for personal success can never be completely fulfilled. We discover that the achievement of the moment may be satisfying for a time, but the elation soon wears off and we become anxious again to attain one more.

Recognizing the enigma does not mean that we are forced to make a trade off, that we must choose between peace of mind and success. However, it does require understanding that our life is not meant to be measured by the size of our collection of personal successes. Peace of mind and the incentive to be successful coexist when we include others in our vision of success, when its meaning is unselfish, when success is more to us than personal attainment. It is the attitude of selflessness, the realization that giving, rather than collecting, is the purpose of our life's activities.

CARING

And I have felt
A presence that disturbs me with the joy
Of elevated thoughts; a sense sublime
Of something far more deeply infused,
...[that] rolls through all things.
                                    —*William Wordsworth*

My coming of age was not accompanied by a solemn ritual or a joyous ceremony—yet the moment remains an emotionally vivid mural. I was an innocent fifteen-year-old, leaning on the wall of a bank at a downtown Sutter Street bus stop, waiting for the #3 Jackson to take me home. In front of me, standing at the curb, a well-dressed middle-aged man lit up his last Marlboro and nonchalantly tossed the flip-top box over his shoulder. It came to rest on its back, its open mouth reflecting my own surprise.

I was stunned—suddenly awakened from my teenage slumber. I couldn't comprehend what I had seen, couldn't believe that a grown man chose to be so blatantly thoughtless to my beloved San Francisco. But I didn't say or do anything. I didn't even pick up the offending empty box. I was afraid of what the businessman might say, the indignant look he might throw my way, or that others at the crowded bus stop would think me foolish to clean up someone else's trash. I did not want to appear "uncool."

Coming at just the right time, initiation experiences reveal the mysteries and elevate the awareness of the neophyte. Until that moment, I hadn't recognized the indifference of so many people to the world around them, believing all adults naturally behaved as responsible citizens. In addition, I was unaware of the extent of my own concern for not creating a messy world, a mess that someone else would have to clean up. Was it just my mother's daily reminder, "Don't forget to clean up your room," or did my feeling arise from something more fundamental?

Since that day sixty years ago, I have often thought about the likely consequences of this and similar acts of carelessness. My reflections have clarified a prosaic but important fact of life: the benefits of our world, including the benefits of a free and well-ordered society, can only be appreciated and supported by those who care. In our sophistication, caring is judged boring and not worth our time. In addition to that delusion, we think that we can get away with not caring, that we can enjoy the benefits without making the effort that accompanies caring. Too many of us fail to see that it is our *not caring* for the various dimensions of our world—community, environment, work, personal relationships—that leads to dissatisfaction.

Who then do we blame for dissatisfaction when it arrives? Since we are not readily inclined to blame ourselves for our unhappiness, we accuse the other guy, arguing that society has deprived us of our fundamental, inherent right of enjoyment. But the truth is that we deprive ourselves.

True enjoyment—not one-dimensional excitement—is inherent in caring. They are what might be called *mutually inclusive*. Caring includes determination, responsibility, involvement—and usually some work. The resulting experience, learning, and sharing creates confidence and satisfaction. But when we lack the will to take care of something or someone, resistance rushes in to fill the gap. What follows is the invention of reasons—rationalization—for not caring. Its accomplice is alienation, the shadow of resistance.

How can we learn to care? How can we encourage others to care? It starts with having a "big picture" of our world, a view larger than our own personal life. We need to select our wide-angle lens if we want to get the true picture. A small self-portrait cannot reveal to us the world that is so full of great benefit. What is this wide-angle lens? Among other things, it is often called *heart*.

It is fear that closes down the lens of our heart, fear of disappointment and uncomfortable emotions. But caring can take place in us only when we allow ourselves to be touched by people and experiences. We cannot care if we are frozen by fear, nor can we enjoy the benefits of our world. Big experiences come to a big heart. It is the only way we can let ourselves be open to others and to various heart-warming possibilities.

I have heard that we should have the heart of the giraffe, because the giraffe has the largest heart of all animals. And I have heard that we should not have the small heart of the jackal. An appropriate metaphor and good advice, since the graceful, peaceful giraffe has a very wide view of the world, embracing vast horizons and great diversity. The jackal runs with his nose to the ground, seeing only what is in front of his face. Their respective worldviews are vastly different.

FEARLESSNESS

*You will always exist in the universe
in some form.*

—*Shunryu Suzuki*

Though too much fear can close our hearts to the world around us, some fear is both natural and necessary—like eating and sleeping. Without the fear of danger—immediate or potential—we would lack caution and life would be brief. So we need not feel ashamed in fearing a threat to our well being—it is a rational response. However, if fear is not to overwhelm our life and rob it of meaning, we need to understand the meaning of our life.

A while ago, the *San Jose Mercury News* carried an article by a writer whose son was in the process of trying out for his high school football team. The father acknowledged that football was dangerous, noting three recent football-caused deaths. Yet his point was that the violence of football was a "test," that it asks its potential players, "Can you conquer the fear? Can you find the courage...that takes you beyond those who are bigger, better, faster?" His point: courage and confidence in our own capacities can be gained by facing up to difficult, intimidating tasks and situations—climbing a mountain, exploring the unknown, fighting a battle.

Yet there is a distinction between courage in the face of danger or threat, when the heart pounds and the adrenalin flows, and true freedom from fear in the ordinary hours and tasks of daily life. With courage, we overcome an "external enemy," whereas freedom from fear, the quality of fearlessness, results from understanding that the real "enemy" is fear of losing what is only temporarily ours. It is not necessary to engage in violence to become fearless.

We cannot know with certainty what will happen in the next moment, the next hour, the next year, or after our life has ended. And so we need to be ready to respond to anything that may happen, to any situation that may confront us, to be prepared to let go of any or all of the things we cherish and work so hard to possess. They may be taken from us without warning: our health, material possessions, love, safety, reputation, comfort, even life itself. Trusting our own readiness is based on understanding that there is something more important in life to take care of than what we are constantly at risk of losing. It is here we establish the meaning of fearlessness.

People who willingly put their own comfort or safety at risk for the benefit of others understand this meaning. They recognize that humanity is not simply a collection of separate individuals going their own separate ways. Rather, it is a community, in the largest sense, of thoughtful people entrusted with the responsibility of caring for each other and for sharing that responsibility.

The source of irrational fear, the kind that leads to suffering, is attachment to ideas and mental constructs about "our self." It leads us to try to preserve the "self," variously known as the ego or the personality. By contrast, spiritual practice directs us toward fearlessness, not by *preserving* but by *understanding*, through experiencing the Reality of things. This understanding comes in the recognition that the end of the "self" is not the end of Reality, that it is an "end" only in a very small sense. Fearlessness is a result of understanding the continuation, not of the "small self," but rather of what we can tentatively call the "larger self" or "big self." The "small self" comes and goes in many forms: the "big self" continues on and on.

True fearlessness is the foundation of the spiritual life. It is not about "overcoming" or conquering the external world. Like happiness, it is not obtained by material gain. It is about maintaining equanimity in each activity, even in the midst of fear or a life-threatening danger. It is expressed when we are fully engaged in the present, even if it is our final moment.

NEVER OUT OF STOCK

It's rather embarrassing...to have given one's entire life to pondering the human predicament and to find out that in the end one has little more to say than "Try to be a little kinder."
—*Aldous Huxley*

Without a clear idea of what we were searching for, my wife and I spent an afternoon shopping for a gift for a friend's birthday. Desperate to find some inspiration, we stopped in a local stationary store. As we entered, we exclaimed almost in unison, "That's it!"

Displayed on the counter were several pen and pencil sets. Hardly concealing my pleasure at our good fortune, I asked the sales clerk to show us the set in black with gold trim.

"Just a moment," she said. "I'll get a new one from the inventory."

She went through a door on our right, into the stockroom. She returned in a few minutes.

"Sorry, we don't have that one."

We examined other items in the display case and asked to look at another set.

"OK, I'll be right back," she told us, and disappeared once more.

She returned empty-handed again, explaining, "We're out of that one, too."

We repeated the scene a third time with the same result.

As we finally turned to leave, the embarrassed clerk tried to let us know she was on our side:

"I don't know why they don't keep the stock up."

Long-term success in business, as well as in life, depends on following a few basic principles. One is, "Don't make promises you can't keep." Its corollary: "Don't offer to provide what you don't have." Breaking this obvious rule risks losing the trust of the people most important to us. It is not limited to a select group; it is everyone we meet—anyone who comes across our threshold. To all of them we need to make available what we have to offer.

Some years ago, the U.S. Army used the recruiting slogan: "Be all that you can be." How can we deny that this simple statement expresses perhaps the most important principle for living a satisfying life: to do what we are able to do according to our abilities and interests and at the same time go beyond our present skills, to learn to do more. By developing new capabilities, our life becomes fuller, adding to the "inventory" we can offer to ourselves and to others.

Without creating a slogan, spiritual practice provides the same kind of encouragement, but with a different emphasis: "Be who you already are." It includes not only being who we can be in the everyday sense, but goes beyond our practical skills to remind us to pay attention to who we are in the wider, universal sense of our inherent bodhisattva nature.

The foundation of Zen practice is its emphasis on our stock of bodhisattva qualities. Unlike the neighborhood store or the shop in the mall, our shelves are always filled; they can never be depleted, we can never run out. This is the foundation of spiritual understanding. Our practice is to make them available to ourselves and to each other. When our life is guided by this recognition, we will not have the feeling, "I have run out." Life remains buoyant, even though our efforts in day-to-day activities do not always succeed.

Making our best effort to be successful in our endeavors is vital if we are to have a satisfying life. But if the goal of success, rather than making our best effort, becomes the overriding concern, we will forget about being our self, forgetting to offer what we already have. Instead, if we orient our life around successful results, we may be tempted to offer what we do not have and will fail to feel satisfaction in what we already have to offer.

Zen practice asks us to reach for the highest of our self throughout life. Not in the usual sense of an objective goal, it is our spiritual "highest," beyond any form of measurement, a life that expresses our inherent positive qualities. These qualities are not something we need to attain; they come with our being born into the world as an expression of something greater than our personality or what we call our "self." They express our fundamental nature. We just have to be awake to them. However, without spiritual practice, we forget who we are, we lose sight of our greater self, and we lose our way. It's as if our inventory has become all jumbled up. We can't find anything, so we don't feel like we have anything.

Selfless meditation practice helps us avoid becoming jumbled up, helps retain an understanding of who we are, and as a result, to have confidence in our fundamental qualities. So if we understand that we are inherently patient, for example, then having patience is not a problem; everything that we need is always at hand. It is impossible to run out of stock.

LOVE IN THE LARGER SENSE

Anyway, I keep picturing all these little kids playing some game in this big field of rye and all. Thousands of little kids, and nobody's around—nobody big, I mean—except me. And I'm standing on the edge of some crazy cliff. What I have to do, I have to catch everybody if they start to go over the cliff—I mean if they're running and they don't look where they're going I have to come out from somewhere and catch them. That's all I do all day. I'd just be the catcher in the rye and all. I know it's crazy, but that's the only thing I'd really like to be.

—*J.D. Salinger*

During a recent public seminar, a young man asked, "What does Buddhism have to say about love?"

Here is a question of the early days of one's spiritual practice, when people are trying to understand how the teachings and the practice fit into their everyday lives. Overwhelmed with first impressions of an intriguing but unfamiliar worldview, they want to know if there is a place for human emotions in the contemplative practice of Zen, with its emphasis on nonattachment. They really want to know: "Will I have to give up love?"

In Buddhism, love has a different starting point than the notion of love prevalent today in Western societies. In countries whose origins are European, love begins with oneself. Personal and romantic, it is aroused by desire for another, often idealized, person. As we commonly understand and accept it, this form of love is motivated by our own need for fulfillment and gratification.

It begins with attraction for someone, a person embodying qualities that delight us—alluring features that, could we embrace and possess them, promise to fill a need in us, to make us whole. And we do need others in this way—we need to relate intimately with one another so that we can feel complete in our lives. The emotion of love is often the catalyst. However, the direction of this form of love is toward our self when it is conditioned by desire. From a spiritual standpoint, it is only a partial understanding of the meaning of love.

Buddhist scriptures do not speak directly about love. But when we start meditation practice, the direction of our feelings starts to shift. Slowly it turns away from emphasis on our self and our desires toward the needs and well-being of others. As the reorientation continues, the feeling of selflessness increases and personal ideas of love lose their powerful grip on our emotions. The mind's view expands.

Rather than personal fulfillment, selflessness emphasizes relationships, through recognition of the interdependency of all things. Buddhist love, therefore, is our experience of the oneness—of the fundamental nature—of all things in the universe.

The teachings of Buddhism are based on compassion. Through meditative practice, the mind becomes calm, balanced, and unselfish, displacing excitement and self-orientation. Our "desire" becomes global, universal, seeking benefit for everyone, rather than for our self alone. Buddhist love, expressed through the words, actions, and presence that we bring to each personal relationship and to each activity, is the expression of our shared sacred nature. It is based on mindfulness, for when we do things with complete attention, we will do them caring for the ways our actions affect each other and our world. If mindfulness is lacking, our concerns remain limited to our self. Our activities and relationships with each other are then at risk for creating problems, leaving messy and noisy traces, rather than expressing care. True love—in the universal sense—must be mature; it cannot be based on childish gratification. It asks us to let go of our own desires, our personal wishes and ideas of like and dislike, to emphasize instead giving our self to others, as a parent to a child.

Buddhist love is expressed in the ways we communicate. Shunryu Suzuki expressed it this way:

> When you listen to someone, you should give up all your preconceived ideas and your subjective opinions; you should just listen to him, just observe what his way is…. We just see things as they are with him, and accept them. This is how we communicate with each other.

At times, we will find our self talking to someone who we sense is troubled by something in his or her life. The concern may be very complex, the other person not able to express it well. If we cannot understand the basis for the unhappiness, we may become confused by what our friend says. And if we are self-oriented, our confusion will develop into irritation and impatience. But through awareness that increases with meditation practice, we enhance our capacity to note the arising of our confusion and to use it as a signal to return to mindfulness. Then we can pay careful attention to the other person, listening for threads, following them back to the source of the feeling, enabling us to respond with care.

Buddhist practice does not discourage the emotional, personally intimate love that is a necessary part of human life. Rather, it encourages love in a larger sense, by cultivation of a loving mind, through awareness and selflessness. We can appreciate it when we allow our mind to expand its view of love, to enable compassion to take its place alongside passion.

THE SOURCE OF COMPASSION

*Morality only is eternal. All the rest is balloon
and bubble from the cradle to the grave.*

                         —John Adams

Wars cover the earth. Everywhere, angry
people continue to persecute and harm
one another: country against country,
religion against religion, people against people, culture against culture. This global illness is not unique
to the modern world. History shows that hostility has
always been part of human societies. Concerned people struggle to find political solutions, but these are
never permanent. A situation changes, a delicate balance is disturbed.

A more lasting resolution occurs when antago-
nists have a change of heart, when they see each
other through new eyes. This shift takes place when

emotional priorities are reoriented from self to other. Then fighting stops and compassion awakens.

Yet how can we be compassionate when we feel oppressed or attacked, frightened or grieving? How can we respond with a caring that enables us to live in peace with each other? What is the fundamental basis for knowing what to do in complex emotional situations?

Religious beliefs provide guidelines for behaving kindly toward one another, as well as for peace of mind. But when passions arise, guidelines are quickly forgotten. Something deeper than belief—the spiritual life—has to be put in play.

A spiritual life requires the gathering of life. It emphasizes focusing attention and activity on what we are doing in the immediate moment, without ideas of personal gain. When we are completely present in that way, each activity becomes the most important activity of our life and every activity—each moment—becomes our entire life.

Individuals who live "saintly" lives inspire us with their continuous spiritual practice, reflected in everything they do. They create nonviolent responses to aggression. They are unconcerned with pursuing personal happiness; their "happiness" is universal, fulfilled by reaching out to others unconditionally. To us, they are the embodiment of compassion. But such people have a sense of something even more basic than compassion.

Compassion is our response to suffering, an emotion followed by action. When we encounter great suffering, compassion is awakened and we are moved to act to relieve the pain. It is awakened because we feel something more fundamental. It is a subtle feeling—present, but not expressed in any overt way in the usual activities of daily life. The many faces of suffering—illness, hunger, death, injustice, oppression—stir this subtle feeling. Then we behave with kindness, courage, and charity. Then we are the saint and we are the bodhisattva. This subtle feeling is our reverence for life.

Mystics of all religious traditions tell us that every activity is the functioning of the divine, of the sacred. Without this understanding we learn to believe that what we do is our own personal activity. When that happens, we place a personal value and a personal importance on our actions. With ideas of "importance," and "me," and "mine," any activity is at risk for going wrong. It can result in competition and fighting because each of us holds differing, often stubborn views of what is "important." If we are to let go our grasp of such ideas and reconcile the separation, we need to understand that in an important way there is no "me" involved.

To have reverence for all things is to express the universal activity in everything we do, to know that all people, things, and activities are spiritual and sacred. They are each worthy to be treated with reverence and taken care of with careful attention.

Offering incense during a religious ceremony, we take care to place it straight—one way to express reverence. Sitting in meditation with straight back and a mind free of ideas of personal gain, we express reverence. To be honest and fully engaged in each activity, without concern for personal payoff, or thinking, "I am doing something special," is reverence in action.

To have universal peace, we first need to have the universal understanding of whose activity is taking place, of who is doing "something special." Suzuki Roshi put it this way,

> When we repeat "I create, I create, I create," soon we forget who is the "I" which creates the various things…. This is the danger of human culture.

When we don't know who we are or what we are doing, the fighting starts. However, by being unattached to what we might gain from our actions, we can know the true value of our activity. Then whatever we do will be guided by reverence.

We can be enlightened in our search for political solutions to human problems if we know that they will be temporary and that the searching is itself Buddha's, or God's, activity. Continuing this understanding in ordinary activities expresses reverence and makes possible the appearance of compassion.

SPIRITUALITY AND TECHNOLOGY

Science...requires an imagination and courage which are not dissimilar to religious creativity. Like the prophet or the mystic, the scientist also forces himself to confront the dark and unpredictable realm of uncreated reality.

—Karen Armstrong

Fifty years ago, Zen practice in Santa Clara Valley—the "Valley of Heart's Delight"— began in a garage of a private home. Over the years, the area became known as "Silicon Valley," famous as the region where industries start in a garage, where major technical breakthroughs are made by one or two individuals working alone. Today it is admired not just for its creation of technology but also for the growth of its economy and the opportunities for its residents.

As Silicon Valley developed, Zen practice also came out of the garage, continuing to grow and become more available. Today an increasing number of people are discovering how to incorporate both scientific, rational thinking and meditation practice into their busy lives. So it is useful to explore the relationship between spiritual practice and technology. What are their similarities and differences? Does spiritual practice help technology and the economy, or do they just share the same terrain?

Meditation is often dismissed as mere self-absorption, opposed to the dynamic activities of work and technology development that emphasize improving the economy and external way of life. Contemplative practice does not analyze; it stresses understanding the universal rather than the particular, our cosmic "Self" rather than our everyday self. Science, or technology, on the other hand, does not explore the "Self," but rather discrete elements of the external, material world. It would appear that they have no relation to each other. However, looking closer, we can understand that they are not in conflict but rather have a number of similarities and actually complement one another.

Both start with self-interest. The meditator hopes to deepen her understanding of life as well as resolve personal questions, perhaps lifelong concerns, even crises. And the scientist, the visionary, and the entrepreneur begin the same way, pursuing an idea of personal interest and challenge.

The true scope of contemplative, spiritual practice is very wide, its nature inclusive of everyone and everything. Its vision is to benefit the entire world. In the same way, successful technical innovation—by standing the test of the marketplace—promises to bring benefit to many. Meditation practice and technology both start with the individual and extend to the world at large.

Spiritual practice is not opposed to the activities of science. Rather, it encourages the continuation of awareness in every activity, whether it is developing a new microchip or washing dishes. The attitude is always the same—to express the authentic, true self in everything we do, no matter what the activity. The key point is to realize what we are doing with our effort in a very large sense.

The activities of science and technology are considered to be "creative." Usually, we understand creativity as bringing some new *thing* into the world. However, if we understand our creativity just in that way, it will be understood in a narrow sense and there is a danger of emphasizing only the personal value, or economic value, of our creation. And we will have a limited understanding of what we are doing, or expressing, because creativity includes more than bringing material things to the marketplace.

Something cannot come from nothing. Any new creation must come from what is available, what is here. The basis of creativity is the vision to see how individual things and people that already exist can give up their unique identity and collaborate to become something new. This means that creativity is based on the relationships of all things to one another: people, objects, the entire world. When we see creativity in that way, it has a very wide meaning, not limited to evolving material technology or works of art.

Spiritual practice and technology have the same foundation. They both invite us to have a mind continuously ready for change, to be intolerant of stubbornness. They discourage clinging to comfortable ways of looking at situations, to risk exploring the unknown, to tolerate uncertainty and ambiguity, and to be accepting of disappointment. Both require—demand—that we not be attached to old ways of doing things, nor to old beliefs, old habits, or old responses. Both encourage readiness for new possibilities and to see opportunities in the midst of difficulties.

When technology is based on spiritual practice, the scope of its creativity is expanded because it then considers a wide range of relationships, not just those that benefit a few. The result is a technology that reflects a taking-care attitude of our community and our world, minimizing the risk of unintended consequences. If an advance in technology solves one problem but creates another, if it improves lives in one place but diminishes it elsewhere, it cannot be called creative, even though it may include a clever design.

Like spirituality, science includes the unscientific relationship of people. There is interdependence between organizations, between companies, and between individual people and organizations. These relationships are always shifting and changing. So a creative environment emphasizes working together in a changing world where many interests and specialties must cooperate. Holding on to a self-oriented view stifles creativity and technology. Developing harmonious relationships in the midst of change encourages invention. This is how spiritual practice is expressed in daily life.

Meditation, as spiritual practice, and technology are ultimately co-dependent. The new century calls for us to balance technical creativity with communal, interpersonal, and global creativity. This includes the relationships of physical things as well as the relationship of people and the environment. It is how we continue spiritual practice in the world of science; it is the true meaning of creativity.

True creativity includes reflecting on the landscape of the world we are creating with our technology, to wonder about the tradeoffs, the gains in standard of living opposed to the receding of a reverential, intimate orientation toward life.

Huston Smith describes our current situation this way:

In different ways, the East and the West are going through a single common crisis whose cause is the spiritual condition of the modern world. That condition is characterized by loss—the loss of religious certainties and of transcendence with its larger horizons. The nature of that loss is strange but ultimately quite logical. When, with the inauguration of the scientific worldview, human beings started considering themselves the bearers of the highest meaning in the world and the measure of everything, meaning began to ebb and the stature of humanity to diminish. The world lost its human dimension, and we began to lose control of it.

On a recent walk downtown, my wife and I noticed another couple walking ahead of us. They were holding hands, an expression of intimacy. At the same time, he was talking on a cell phone at his right ear, while her cell phone was held to her left. With eyes averted from each other and attention directed to the remote "other," their affection and intimacy was replaced by indifference.

If we allow technology to make us less mindful of each other, we diminish the quality of our relationships—our capacity to listen and respond with attentiveness and feeling—and, in a subtle way, our trust of one another.

We isolate ourselves, losing touch with our spiritual nature.

LIFE IS NOT A COMMODITY

I believe a leaf of grass is no less than the
    journey work of the stars,
And the pismire is equally perfect, and a grain
    of sand, and the egg of a wren,
And the tree toad is a chef-d'oeuvre for the
    highest,
And the running blackberry would adorn the
    parlors of heaven...

            —*Walt Whitman*

The ancient Zen challenge to "make a sixteen-foot high golden Buddha from a blade of grass" points to the sacred nature of the everyday world, completely expressing the heart of spirituality. Underlying the expression is the insight that neither living beings nor inanimate objects are separate from the sacred, or however we choose to refer to the universal nature of our existence.

Transforming grasses into Buddhas does not require us to master an enigmatic, mystical secret. Its source is close at hand, immediate: our respect for all things, especially the attention we give to the least glamorous stuff of everyday life. It means treating everything with the same respect we would pay to whatever we hold sacred. To pay reverence to some special religious sacredness is in some sense easy. To feel reverence for a blade of grass, a bug, or a rock requires the intention and attentiveness of spiritual practice.

We turn to spiritual practice when we sense the unreality of the world of commodities. We long to know the world of true Reality, to live according to the truth of life, not according to desires. We perceive that life is not a commodity but rather a gift, that fundamentally it is not something for our personal "use." Seeing people, nature, and the things that come into our life as commodities causes us to treat them in a careless way. And it follows that we then treat our own life carelessly, not understanding why we feel confused and off balance. If we are not careful—if we do not pay attention—we will see the world as a commodity and we will become like a commodity our self. This is how life loses its meaning.

While I was visiting a patient in the hospice of the Veterans Hospital in Palo Alto, the head nurse came to his room to see how he was doing. He said to her, "When will I die?" He was not in pain and his mind was still sharp and active. Yet he felt useless, and he suffered from the feeling. He knew his body was wearing out, that he could no longer do the things that gave independence and satisfaction to his once active and robust life. He was now almost totally dependent on others. And so he felt, "This commodity is worn out, my life is useless."

So often we find satisfaction only in our usefulness, in our ability to help each other and make things work.

Deprived of that capacity, we may suffer. But *usefulness* is not the sole reason for having life. In each moment, we have the capacity to do our best, to treat our life with respect with whatever capacity we have at that moment. We can be Buddha in every moment—a big capacity Buddha or a small capacity Buddha; it makes no difference.

We find joy in life when we pay respect to the capacity we have, even when it is diminished, even when we are left with just our breath. We find it when we appreciate that each capacity—just like each thing or person—is a gift, not a commodity. In meditation, we limit our activity to awareness of our breath, while we let go of ideas such as "useful" and "productive." Simply maintaining awareness of our breath allows us to see everything and everyone as a gift.

Each effort we make becomes a gift—and respect for all of life spontaneous—when we see how everything that comes our way is a gift. Tiring of striving for commodities, we begin our search for the truth of things and we are ready for spiritual practice. It begins with full awareness of the smallest things—our breath, a blade of grass. Then the breath and the grass are themselves holy. And whatever capacity we have at that moment is also holy. Spiritual practice means not going to the shopping mall in our head, not trying to find souvenirs for our mind. Rather, spiritual practice aims at seeing the true meaning of each thing and of each effort, independent of size or usefulness. This is how a blade of grass becomes Buddha.

No transformation is necessary.

SANCTUARY

To that still center where the spinning world
Sleeps on its axis, to the heart of rest.
                                        —Dorothy L. Sayers

A t the heart of religion and spiritual practice rests a vision of sanctuary. Without this feeling, a religion, or practice, has limited meaning. For centuries, sanctuary has meant a physical place of safety, free from danger, providing comfort and support. At the same time, it is a place where one acknowledges and feels connection to something larger, universal, that can be trusted. Sanctuary is where the sacred is touched and honored. Taking refuge in sanctuary brings peace and calm.

In Zen practice, sanctuary is not concerned with a physical place, such as a church, meditation hall, cave, or forest grove. In this practice, sanctuary resides within each of us. It exists when we have the mind of practice, where there is no feeling of being unsafe or unprotected. Because the feeling of connection to something larger is present, distinction between self and sacred dissolves. This is the mind of sanctuary.

When our analytical, discriminating, or grasping mental activity is quiet, our small mind does not disturb itself, and big mind, or Buddha's mind, can be expressed. According to Buddhism, everyone is inherently endowed with Buddha's mind, and so sanctuary is everywhere, in every activity, even in the midst of difficulty and suffering. When the mind is quiet—empty of striving—it is not overwhelmed by anxiety, the oppressive fear of losing something. This mind understands that it can never lose what is vital.

Sitting in meditation, our mind is given a chance to be calm and quiet. Even if just for a few minutes between periods of distraction, we get a glimpse and understand something of big mind. This subtle understanding lets us know that Buddha mind is always taking care. Practice is how we are supported by the mind that is not overwhelmed by the difficulties of life. When we try too hard to gain something or hold on to something, we lose that feeling of support, we lose sight of what is vital. Instead, we feel threatened, unsafe, and search outside of our self for sanctuary. With practice, we discover the inherent support that we always have, that we cannot lose, that we don't have to ask for. With this feeling and understanding we have no need to seek support from outside of our self. Spiritual practice is the way we learn to rely on our self, our big self, how we return to the center of our existence. This center is not a thing or place; it is our big mind, our true nature, which is never contaminated by doubt, fear, or confusion.

To return to the center is to arrange our life, like a well-rehearsed orchestra, which has many different instruments, all with unique sounds. When arranged, the orchestra creates music that is more than a collection of separate sounds. It expresses something much greater. When you listen to the orchestra, you cannot listen to just one instrument, even if you have a favorite. You have to give up trying to hear each part separately; otherwise there is confusion and you become lost in noise. Before a concert, musicians tune up individually. The sound is chaotic, noisy. Someone has to arrange the orchestra, organize the separate parts, or chaos continues. If you feel confused and lost in noise, it means you are not listening to the big sound, as if the orchestra is not arranged, out of harmony, as if the conductor has left the stage and each instrument is doing its own thing.

Spiritual practice is how we bring the conductor on stage by returning to the empty mind that quiets things down and allows them to arrange themselves.

If we want to organize and arrange our self and our life, we need to have humility, not a humility of subservience, of concern about what people think of us, or of feeling that our life has little value. Rather, it is the creative humility arising from the confidence of knowing who we are in the largest sense. It is understanding why and how it is necessary to arrange our self with others. Without humility, we continually insist on our own way, insist on playing our personal instrument. Without the humility that arises from confidence, we will not understand the need to hear others, to be in harmony with others, and so be supported by others. But with this humility, we exist in sanctuary.

To practice with each other is to be arranged with each other without the need to say too much. Practice does not rely on our words; we communicate at a deeper level, like instruments in an arranged orchestra. Activities in the meditation hall are harmonious: sitting together and walking together, bowing, chanting, and working together. We have no idea of our own individuality. Our emphasis is on paying attention to what is going on, always considering, "How can I arrange my effort with everyone?" This humility supports our life and the lives of all others.

Something very big is going on in this world. In spiritual practice we enter into the big activity that is larger than our individual self and is always in arrangement. Our practice is to organize our self and our life according to big mind and not be troubled by the chaos of a self-oriented mind. Practice is the sanctuary of big mind.

SUBTLETY

When, with breaking heart,
I realize
This world is only a dream,
The oak tree looks radiant.

—*Anryu Suharu*

Zen emphasizes understanding the true nature of all conditioned phenomena of the world we live in, including, mainly, ourselves. We usually begin by reading and listening to others, trying to intellectually absorb the various Buddhist teachings of transiency, impermanence, and "no self," the insights into how the human mind creates its own suffering, and how we can gain clarity and peace. Reflecting on these ideas helps the mind appreciate things with a new perspective, not simply according to appearances or what "common sense" presents. However, being limited to the intellect, the ideas are not enough to bring about true understanding. It takes place only when our inherent, subtle wisdom—hidden from thinking or analysis—expresses itself.

I can still recall my first lesson about the value of understanding through subtlety. It happened sometime around age twelve, on a warm, spring Saturday afternoon, the highlight of the week for my friends and me. In our boisterous New York manner, we raced up Broadway to the local movie theater to watch an action film about the crusades. Halfway through the drama of politics and romance, the armies of King Richard and Saladin, Sultan of Egypt, prepare for war. The two leaders meet in Richard's tent on the evening of the battle. Attempting to impress his adversary with the might of the Christian army, Richard brings down his heavy-duty English sword onto a large block of metal, smashing it in two with a great crash. Saladin, unimpressed with the king's dramatics, responds, "You have shown us the strength of your arm, not the sharpness of your steel." Saladin then draws his narrow scimitar. An attendant tosses a silk scarf in the air. As it descends, Saladin holds out his blade and with a slight upward movement of his arm, the flimsy fabric is severed without resistance.

Like many films of those days, it was corny Hollywood stuff. But for me, it illustrated an often-overlooked truth: subtlety has the quality of sharpness, it "cuts through" without force and without fighting. My young mind, conditioned to movies and newsreels of the battles, noise, and explosiveness of World War II, was impressed by the demonstration of quiet "cutting through."

The principle holds true for a mind as well as a sword. Giving it a chance to be still gives it a chance to be sharp, to enable composure and wisdom to arise. It is the experiential way, allowing the busy mind to feel its basic quality, beyond the conglomerate, noisy things of the everyday world. It is the subtle way of seeing the world, including oneself and others. Without this subtlety, worldly things seem to us to be inherently either "attractive" or "unattractive." This arbitrary mental distinction in turn creates either desire or repulsion. Known in Buddhism as duality, it is the source of confusion and anxiety.

By contrast, attentive stillness yields insight into nondistinction—unexciting in an everyday sense, but subtly revealing and joyous.

TRUE CREATIVITY

I go to prove my soul!
I see my way as birds their trackless way.
—Robert Browning

T rue creativity must include our personal effort, as well as a certain kind of excitement—quiet, born from a vision of one's self in the world, from having a sense of purpose for each individual act. It comes from seeing the larger value of a single activity, beyond personal or material value, accompanied by the feeling, "This is a good thing to do." Without this quiet feeling, it is difficult for daily tasks to feel creative in a large sense.

At the same time, the creative life includes things that we are drawn to, that we admire, that we intuitively feel express our own true value, the unmeasurable measure of our self beyond market value or exchange value. It is a mistake to keep such things at arms length, if we feel drawn or touched, even if they seem foreign, too much trouble, uncomfortable, or in the way of personal ambition. A full life must include the things we feel express our true value.

No one can force another person to engage in spiritual practice. It is also impossible to force our self. We will practice only when we feel it expresses our true value, our fundamental essence. So we shouldn't try to force it on our self or anyone else if there is no deep feeling. On the other hand, if the feeling is there, we should practice, not just admire it from afar. At least, we should make our best effort. Otherwise, we are not being true to our self, to our own feelings of what is a life of true creativity and true value. It is a tragedy to ignore our own wisdom. It is what used to be called "Selling your soul to the devil."

It is not unusual to be a little excited when we first feel we can embrace the activity of true value. We may even feel, "At last!"—like the excitement of a thirsty man finding water. Later, our feelings become less excited, more natural, just as water is simply what we drink when thirsty.

Then when we find it, it is nothing special.

WE ARE NEEDED

But because truly being here is so much;
because everything here apparently needs us,
this fleeting world which in some strange way
keeps calling to us.

—Rainer Maria Rilke

Rilke's "Ninth Duino Elegy" nudges us to reconsider our reason for being. We are urged to shed the pervading attitude, to perceive our world in terms of "other," rather than in terms of "self." But it is not easy to disavow generations of long-held beliefs, nor to radically transform a lifetime of cherished convictions.

In its desperate need to find itself, humanity turns to religion and spiritual practice. We want to leap beyond a troublesome sense of insignificance and isolation, to find the bridge to our True Self and recognize the source of our being. We want to associate our belonging with something larger than the ordinary. We want to belong—at last—in a natural, unforced way. Exhausted from the effort, we want to end the endless, lifelong struggle. We are wearied of feeling like a stranger in our own skin and on our own turf.

Not feeling included in something larger, we feel, instead, something wrong—unfair—as if we are forcibly being kept apart from our True Self. Rilke's insight tells us it is not so: the world is waiting to welcome us; we are not estranged. Our confusion arises from not awakening to what is going on. The world is not keeping us at a distance; it is just that we have to actively engage our life in a personal effort of welcoming.

In contemplative spiritual practice, we sit in silence and awareness, giving our attention to the larger world, the world without the limits of time or space, words, or thoughts. This is the fundamental act of welcoming. Through the practice of awareness we discover harmony with the all-inclusive world that once seemed outside our personal borders. Subtly we recognize, "This is it—my turf is everywhere."

In this recognition the boundary between world and self evaporates, our imaginary restraints dissolve. Gone are the illusory frontier barrier gates and guard posts; our "cold war" is ended. Our sense of separation is replaced by a feeling of coming home, of belonging. We no longer have a desperate need for explanations. We understand why we are needed, and we understand how to fulfill our role of taking care of our world.

Taking care has many forms. It does not always require rushing into a situation to resolve a problem. At the start of a recent meditation retreat, a young woman began sobbing softly. Nobody moved; everyone continued sitting quietly. After a few minutes, the sobbing stopped. To an outside observer, this non-response may seem indifferent: no comforting, no solace, no arm around the shoulder. Yet, the non-intervention was "taking care" in a large sense. Following the retreat, the woman who had been sobbing expressed gratitude for support and encouragement, for the opportunity to "find herself."

Taking care begins with being present. It is an expression of oneness, an attitude of reaching out to the world. It requires tearing down fortress walls. Throughout history, cities and nations constructed protective barricades—political and physical—to provide security against a constant threat of invasion. The same is true for individuals. We develop defensive shields against the uncertainties of indifference, cruelty, injustice, and sudden tragedies. Despite our fears, at some point we have to let the walls come down so that we may understand why we have this life and why we are needed.

A well-known Zen story describes how a ninth-century Chinese Zen monk experienced awakening on hearing the sound of a stone striking a bamboo tree as he was sweeping the ground around his hermitage. It is a story of a mind already open, ready to welcome the world, through an attitude of actively taking care. It is a story of setting aside personal concerns so that we may give our self to the world that needs us.

Spiritual practice can seem hard for some people, but the real source of difficulty is not found in any of the usual reasons for a task to be truly hard. It is not about lack of skill or lack of time. To believe "I can't do this" or "I don't have time" is to misunderstand why spiritual practice feels difficult. It feels "hard" because it requires us to let go of self-centered protective barricades and to risk feeling vulnerable to an unseen enemy. But life is not a military action. There is no enemy; defeat exists only in the imagination. To let down our barriers is to let go of our small self, to come back to our True Self, to a deep sense of belonging to something vast, to the transcendental feeling Rilke describes in the poem's final line:

> *Superabundant being wells up*
> *in my heart.*

THE NATURAL WORLD

If you want to reach the true path beyond
doubt,
place yourself in the same freedom as sky.
You name it neither good nor not good.

—Zen Master Nansen

I n the chill of winter, how reassuring to hear the click
and whirr of the central heating system automatically kicking in. In spring and summer, automatic
sprinkler systems in parks and along freeways water
the grass and flowers. At dusk, city streetlights come
on, apparently by themselves. Machines with preset
cycles wash, rinse, and dry our clothes.

We take these things for granted. And with technology advancing every day, we expect a greater part
our lives to become more and more "automatic," to
be taken care of for us. We believe that relief from

these chores provides us the freedom to be creative, to be unconstrained, to be natural.

We have to be careful of going too far "automating" our lives, of separating ourselves from the workings of our world. In our increasingly automatic daily life, remaining involved and intimate is necessary if we are to feel natural. Without our attention to things and people around us, we inhibit our natural expression. If we strive to have all the "troublesome" things of life taken care of for us, relieving us from making a personal effort, we will forget who we are in the larger sense. We will not understand our natural self and will not feel our inherent freedom.

The fundamental, most important, natural activities of life are already "automatic." Dawn comes without our interference. Rain falls. In spring, the garden blooms, the trees leaf out. Yet in many ways, we are part of the natural unfolding. The garden blooming is more than spring arriving. It needs us to take care—to dig, weed, water, and harvest. The seed becomes the fruit or flower automatically; that is its natural function. It does so with the automatic help of the sun and the rain fulfilling their functions. At the same time, its blossoming also includes us, fulfilling our role in the automatic functioning of the natural world.

Life is not just about taking care of our self. It includes taking care of everything, of what we call the big self. It is taking care of the natural world. In

Buddhism it is said, "All things exist in our self." When we have this kind of appreciation for life, we will naturally—without hesitation—take care of all things: our life, the life around us, the entire garden. Without this understanding, we will be concerned only with taking care of *me*. And we will demand that the activities of life that seem to be unrelated to our personal fulfillment be made automatic, entirely taken care of by the world outside. When that happens, we will forget how to take care of things, how to fulfill our function, how to be our natural self. Then there can be no blossoming of our self or others.

Sometimes we actively do something in the garden. At other times, we observe and do not interfere. Both activities are included in "taking care." Sometimes we fix something, or we correct an error. At other times we purposely limit our self to observing an activity, confident that it is going OK without our involvement. Either way, we are "taking care."

Ordinarily we think of freedom as not having to take care of things beyond the range of our own needs and desires. Yet we can only find our freedom within a caretaking attitude, not when life is automated for us. Inherently people are no different than the sun or rain. We have the capacity to take care when we allow ourselves to be natural. If we avoid taking care, we actually go against our true nature and life tilts off balance. We are unable to feel the joy of our natural, big self. As an ancient Zen master declared, "To bear

fruit in other people should be our natural activity."
When we understand the natural way of taking care,
plants bloom through us. And we bloom through
them. It is the same with each other.

To do something—or not do it—in a natural way,
through understanding, without too much thinking,
is the expression of our natural self. Then there is no
separation, not between you and me, not between our
self and the world garden. Natural taking care comes
about when we are fully involved in the present
moment, just as it is being expressed, free from the
distortion of our own desires. Spiritual practice is
how we take care of our "automatic" natural self. It
is the only way to express who we really are.

Spiritual activity is meant to be continued even in
the rush of daily lives. Like the sun, wind, and rain,
we have the capacity to nurture all things, without
exception.

Who can say when or where the next seed will
bloom?

EPILOGUE

Crawl and stop, crawl and stop. Even by nine-thirty in the morning, the manic commute into the city had not yet settled itself into a smooth trajectory. Patience remained essential. On this damp November morning, we were making our tenth consecutive daily trip into San Francisco to teach the final hour of my "Meditation at Work" workshop.

Shellie broke the silence as the city skyline came into view, the sun starting to show through the thinning fog. "How do you think the class is going?" Her voice betrayed a tinge of concern.

"It's hard to say. This group is so different from others."

Shellie had offered to help teach this workshop to a unique group of students in a unique training program. "Step Ahead" was a twenty-eight-week welfare-to-work program co-sponsored by PG&E (Pacific

Gas and Electric), the San Francisco Department of Human Services, City College of San Francisco, and the Women's Foundation of San Francisco. The students, mostly women, including many single mothers, all experiencing stress and uncertainty in their lives, were being taught marketable workplace skills, including word-processing, spreadsheet preparation, and data base maintenance. As part of their sponsorship, PG&E guaranteed a job for at least six months to successful graduates.

I was asked to teach the students a way to reduce stress and maintain composure as they struggled to master new technical skills and to learn how to swim upstream in the daunting, often turbulent corporate world.

"It's not easy for them to sit still," Shellie observed. "There's a lot of fidgeting going on."

"Part of it may be that the class is not voluntary. They're *required* to attend; its part of the whole program they're in," I said, keeping my eye on the on-again-off-again taillights in front of us.

"That's right. I wouldn't want to be told that I had to meditate. I sure would have a lot of resistance. It's something you have to come to on your own."

The conversation paused as we turned off the freeway and headed into downtown. After a few minutes, Shellie spoke up again. "I think one of the biggest difficulties for them is the subtleness of meditation. They don't get any feedback. It's hard for them to tell if they're getting anything from it. For sure, that must be discouraging."

Shellie is a marriage and family therapist specializing in addiction and recovery, working with high-risk teens and their families. She is intimately familiar with the mountainous world of lifelong frustration and discouragement, of the frightening, slippery-cold feelings of hopelessness and isolation. Over the past two weeks, she and I had listened to the stories of our students, trying to find ways to encourage them to sit quietly with an alert posture and to stay aware of their breathing. During the meditation part of the class sessions, many gave up immediately, unable to find a minimum of self-discipline, slumping in their chairs with arms folded, waiting for the twenty minutes to end. Even for those who were giving the practice a chance and making their best effort, I knew it must be frustrating. I wondered if we had done any good, if all the commuting and the effort—ours and theirs—had been worth it.

At the end of class on this final Friday, the students thanked us as we, in turn, wished them well with their studies and their new careers. Then something happened that erased all my doubts.

The last woman to leave the classroom took me by the arm and drew me aside. In her tearful voice, barely audible, I heard relief and gratitude.

"Mr. Kaye," she said, "I don't hit my little boy anymore."

APPENDIX

A BASIC INTRODUCTION TO ZAZEN
SPIRITUAL PRACTICE IN THE ZEN TRADITION

Your straight spine is the most important element of meditation—paradoxically, it should be noted that a "straight spine" includes a natural forward curve in the lower back, with the belly pushed forward slightly. The spine provides the foundation for an upright posture, the prerequisite for an upright mind. It also enables the breath to flow easily and deeply, in and out of the area below the navel.

Ideally, twenty minutes should be the minimum amount of time for meditation. However, there is really no such thing as a minimum amount of time if you spontaneously decide to "sit." You can, for example, meditate on a train or bus. You can take a five-minute meditation break in your office at work. You can just sit quietly and follow your breath for a minute or two, anywhere, anytime, when you notice stress coming on, or just feel a need to regain composure or balance. However, it is very valuable to sit formally with others for larger periods of time; 25–40 minutes is usual at most meditation centers.

POSTURE

The traditional posture for Zen meditation is crosslegged on a cushion. To sit in this way, sit slightly forward on your cushion, slightly forward of the crown. This will enable some of the body weight to be supported by the legs, rather than just the tailbone. The knees and tailbone form the base of a pyramid, the most stable geometric structure.

Cross your legs into the *full-lotus*, *half-lotus*, or *Burmese* position. For full lotus: Place the right ankle on the left thigh and the left ankle on the right thigh. For half-lotus: Place the right ankle on the left thigh and the left ankle under, or in front of, the right knee, or vice versa. For Burmese: Place the right ankle under or in front of the left knee and the left ankle under or in front of the right knee.

If it is not possible to sit cross-legged, you can try sitting in a supported kneeling position—kneeling astride a supporting cushion, like a meditation cushion turned on its edge—or sitting on a special kneeling bench, called a *seiza bench*.

It's also entirely possible to do zazen sitting in a regular chair. This is often the most comfortable posture. And it is "portable" because no special meditation cushion is needed. However, it can feel less stable than the other postures because of the body's higher center of gravity.

To do zazen in a chair: Use a chair without arms, if available. Place feet comfortably on the floor, about shoulder width apart. Remove your shoes, if that is more comfortable. Sit in the center or forward portion of the chair. Try not to lean on the back of the chair. However, if you have some difficulty with your back, you can lean on the back of the chair to relieve chronic discomfort. As much as possible, let your upper body be supported by your straight spine.

After selecting and settling into one of these zazen postures, take a moment to straighten the entire spine. The lower spine should curve in slightly. The straightness of the spine should extend through the top of the head, as if the crown of the skull were supporting the ceiling. This will lower the chin, causing the gaze to be down about thirty to forty-five degrees.

Keep the mouth closed, the tip of the tongue against the teeth. Keep the eyes partially open (one-third to one-half). Even though you may feel that keeping the eyes fully closed is less distracting and more relaxing, it is important to keep them open—along with all the other senses—in order to fully practice awareness. Keep the shoulders back slightly in a confident posture, not slumped forward or strained too far back. Keep the elbows slightly away from the sides. Imagine you are holding a raw egg under each arm: don't break them and don't drop them.

Place the back of the left hand on top of the palm of the right hand, with the palm of the left hand facing up. Keep the fingers together. Rest the hands comfortably on your lap or legs. Let your thumbs touch just slightly, forming an oval.

Take a mental alignment of the body: ears, shoulders and hips in line, tip of nose and navel in line.

BREATHING

Deep breathing is necessary for a calm, stable mind; shallow breathing accompanies anxiety.

Let the breath come in through the nose, allowing it to go deep to the abdomen. The tummy should fill up, pushing forward slightly.

Pause, and when ready, gently guide the breath out through the nose, deflating the tummy.

Pause, and, when ready, let the breath come in again.

Continue breathing in and out slowly. Breathing will slow down to about four or five breathes per minute.

Maintain mental awareness on the inhale, the exhale, and the pause in between.

If the mind wanders, simply return awareness to the breath.

COUNTING THE BREATH

Counting the breath is a technique for helping the mind stay aware when it is extremely restless.

Count the exhales, one through ten, as you finish exhaling. When you reach ten, start over at one.

If you lose count, start over without hesitation. Don't try to remember where you lost track.

Counting is only a temporary aid when very distracted. Put it aside when the mind settles down, when you can count to ten without losing track.

SOME WORDS OF ADVICE

Keeping time. If you do not want to watch the clock, place a kitchen timer in a drawer or closet so that the clicking is muffled but the bell can be heard. The alarm on a digital watch works well. Some people use a lighted stick of incense cut to the correct length to measure the time. After some experience, the body will know when the appropriate time has elapsed and it will be necessary to look at a clock only once or twice.

Commitment. Try to practice zazen every day, whether convenient or not, comfortable or not. Do it even if some obstacles arise. Don't worry about "liking" it, being "bored," "success," or "progress."

Self-discipline. Set aside a certain time of day, preferably morning, very soon after arising, for meditation. If there is resistance to getting out of bed when the alarm rings, quickly put one foot on the floor. The rest of you will find it easier to follow.

INDEX

ABOUT THE AUTHOR

LES KAYE started work in 1958 for IBM in San Jose, California, and over thirty years held positions in engineering, sales, management, and software development. Les became interested in Zen Buddhism in the mid 1960s and started Zen practice in 1966 with a small group in the garage of a private home. In 1970, he took a leave of absence to attend a three-month practice period at Tassajara Zen monastery in California and the following year was ordained as a Zen monk by Zen Master Shunryu Suzuki. In 1973, he took an additional leave of absence to attend a second practice period, this time as head monk, and in 1984, Les received Dharma Transmission, authority to teach, from Hoitsu Suzuki, son and successor to Shunryu Suzuki. He was appointed teacher at Kannon Do Zen Center in Mountain View, California. He and his wife Mary have two adult children and a grandson and live in Los Altos, California. His first book was *Zen at Work*.

WISDOM PUBLICATIONS

To learn more about **WISDOM PUBLICATIONS**, a nonprofit publisher, and to browse our other books dedicated to skillful living, visit our website at www.wisdompubs.org.

You may request a copy of our catalog online or by writing to this address:

Wisdom Publications
199 Elm Street
Somerville, Massachusetts 02144 USA
Telephone: 617-776-7416
Fax: 617-776-7841
Email: info@wisdompubs.org
www.wisdompubs.org

Wisdom is a nonprofit, charitable 501(c)(3) organization affiliated with the Foundation for the Preservation of the Mahayana Tradition (FPMT).